THE STATUS OF BLACKS
IN HIGHER EDUCATION

THE STATUS OF BLACKS IN HIGHER EDUCATION

Ada M. Elam, EdD

Editor

A NAFEO Research Institute Publication Supported By
Grants From
The Carnegie Corporation,
The Charles Stewart Mott Foundation,
The Pew Memorial Trust Company,
and The Rockefeller Foundation.

UNIVERSITY
PRESS OF
AMERICA

Lanham • New York • London

Copyright © 1989 by the

NAFEO Research Institute

University Press of America,® Inc.

4720 Boston Way
Lanham, MD 20706

3 Henrietta Street
London WC2E 8LU England

Printed in the United States of America

British Cataloging in Publication Information Available

Co-published by arrangement with The National
Association for Equal Opportunity in Higher Education

Library of Congress Cataloging–in–Publication data

The Status of Blacks in higher education / Ada M. Elam, editor.
p.   cm.
1.Afro–Americans– –Education (Higher) I. Elam, Ada M. II. NAFEO
Research Institute (U.S.)
LC2781.S72   1988   88–39410 CIP
378'.008996073– –dc19
ISBN 0–8191–7286–3 (alk. paper).
ISBN 0–8191–7287–1 (pbk. : alk. paper)

All University Press of America books are produced on acid-free paper.
The paper used in this publication meets the minimum requirements of American
National Standard for Information Sciences—Permanence of Paper for Printed Library
Materials, ANSI Z39.48–1984.   ∞

Table of Contents

Foreword

What is the state of the higher education of blacks? Researchers at the National Association for Equal Opportunity in Higher Education (NAFEO) and its membership association of 117 historically and predominantly black colleges (HBCUs) have studied scores of statistical series to answer that question. Our examination of these series has left us with some strong convictions. The state of black higher education is good. Indeed, progress in the higher education of blacks until recently has been phenomenal. Currently that progress is stalled. The implementation of wise and sound policies, however, would enable us to regain the lost momentum and continue to expand educational opportunities for blacks. It is essential that we do so not only for blacks but for America as a whole.

In Chapter I, Dr. Lonnie Crosby looks at the current state of blacks in those fields that have been identified by the U.S. Department of Labor as high growth areas for college graduates for 1985–1995: Accountants and Auditors, Computer Programmers, Computer System Analysts, Electrical and Electronic Engineers, Kindergarten and Elementary School Teachers, Lawyers, Mechanical Engineers, Physicians, and Registered Nurses. As Crosby indicates, blacks are not graduating in these areas in large numbers. Because of the underrepresentation of blacks in these areas, this should enhance the black graduate's opportunity for employment, Cosby adds.

According to Dr. Elaine P. Witty, "blacks constitute a smaller percent of teachers in America than was the case six years ago," and the prospects for improving their representation are dismal, hence, the title of her paper in Chapter II, "Teacher Education: Lost Ground for Blacks." She chronicles the pipeline of blacks from high school graduation, through bachelor degree attainment in education, to their small representation in the teaching force. Dr. Witty goes on to discuss three major factors contributing to the small number of blacks and other minorities in the teaching field: 1) a smaller percentage of college students (both black and white) enrolling in teacher education programs, 2) the new thrust/trend toward mandatory tests for admission into teacher education programs and for initial teacher certification, and 3) the educational reform movements calling for an additional year of training in teacher education beyond the bachelor's degree in a specific discipline.

Writing in Chapter III, Dr. Oscar Prater and Ms. Brendoler Miller assess the status of blacks in the professions of law and medicine in reference to the level of parity between blacks as a percentage of these professions and blacks as a percentage of the general population. They further identify the number of blacks needed for parity with the population, the high school graduate rate, and the percentage of college entrants. In the end, they compare the current level of parity with the levels for five and ten years earlier. They conclude that the "status" of blacks in the field of medicine is less favorable today than it was five and ten years earlier. . . . and that "the status of blacks in the field of law is less favorable today than it was five years earlier. . . ."

In the last chapter, "Geographic Mobility Status of Black Women in Higher Education Administration: Selected Parameters," Dr. Hazeltine Woods-Fouche analyzes demographic and professional characteristics of black women in higher education administration at the historically black colleges and universities (HBCUs), their career patterns and aspirations, and their perceptions of factors influencing and inhibiting geographic mobility. Dr. Woods-Fouche concludes that "In the aggregate, black female administrators are employed in the south central region, married, between the ages of thirty and forty-nine, have at least one dependent child, completed their study in the field of education during the 1970's, employed at four-year public HBCU colleges/ universities in middle level positions basically obtained through promotion."

In addition, Dr. Woods-Fouche states that "a substantial proportion of black female administrators are willing to relocate in order to secure advancement," and that ways need to be found to eliminate constraints to geographic mobility.

Ada M. Elam
Bowie State College

Chapter I

Blacks in Various Fields of Study: Implications for Manpower Needs Into the Twenty-First Century

Dr. Lonnie C. Crosby
Assistant V.P. for Academic Affairs
Jackson State University, MS

Looking ahead to manpower needs as related to blacks in the twenty-first century requires the examination of several peripheral factors. This paper is the result of an attempt to determine the present level of participation of blacks in selected fields, to determine the fields that are growth areas, and to determine the related implications for higher education into the next century. In order to address the problem, efforts were made to survey related literature on the subject, to collect data showing the productivity of blacks in higher education fields of study, and to collect data related to manpower needs in the twenty-first century.

The underrepresentation of blacks and other minorities in the better jobs of our society has been widely discussed. The present unsatisfactory status of Blacks in the work force will be exacerbated further without constant vigilance as to what is taking place. In view of some work force projections, certain job opportunities will either cease or become more competitive. The 16-to-24 year-old group of non-whites as a percentage of total workers is projected to rise from 15.5 percent to 18.3 percent by 1990. Furthermore, the 25-to-44 age bracket of the work force is projected to grow to 60.5 million by 1990. This represents a 55 percent increase above the 39 million at this age bracket in 1975. In the 25–44 age group, the competition for the better jobs and for promotions will be intense under conditions of increased supply of the work force. These projections and related data give relevance to the question, "What does this mean for higher education?"

Job Market for College Graduates

Jon Sargent (1986, p. 3), an economist in the Bureau of Labor Statistics (BLS) of the U.S. Department of Labor, has expressed the opinion that "the job market for college graduates finally appears to be improving." Sargent goes further to predict that about 8 out of every 9 graduates who enter the work force between now and 1995 will find a college-level job.

The projections given by Sargent are related to job openings that require four or more years of college; therefore, the junior college graduate was not included here. The demand for four-year college graduates is determined from three sources: (1) growth in the number

2

of jobs that traditionally require a college degree; (2) replacements needed to fill jobs of employed college graduates who leave the labor force; and (3) educational upgrading of jobs formerly performed by people who were not college graduates.

Promising Fields of Employment

Economists in the Bureau of Labor Statistics of the U.S. Department of Labor have developed projections of the number of jobs that will be needed in 1995 by occupation. The BLS actually developed three different projections. The three projections are referred to as low, moderate, and high growth scenarios. The information presented in this paper relates to the moderate projections published in the Spring 1986 issue of the *Occupational Outlook Quarterly*. The article analyzed about 200 of the more than 500 jobs listed in another publication of the BLS. The growth rate of jobs analyzed were viewed two ways: by rate of growth and by absolute numbers.

Rate Growth. In the Spring 1986 issue of *Occupational Outlook Quarterly,* the editor, Neal Baxter, listed the twenty top occupations having the highest projected growth rates. The five fastest growing occupations included in the twenty were paralegal personnel, computer programmers, computer systems analysts, medical assistants, and data processing equipment repairers. Many of the fastest growing occupations are small, employing fewer than 50,000 people. Occupations with small numbers, obviously, cannot provide a larger number of new jobs even with rapid growth rates.

Numbers Growth. The jobs that will show the greatest increase in the absolute number of new jobs are represented by only 37 of the 500 jobs analyzed by BLS. These 37 occupations will account for approximately fifty percent of all job growth between 1984 and 1995. One fourth of these 37 occupations generally require a college degree.

A review of the BLS (Austin, 1986) *Job Outlooks Projections* reveals that 9 of the 37 occupations either obviously require at least a bachelor's degree or a bachelor's degree is needed to enhance one's opportunity for employment. These nine occupations are: registered nurses, accountants and auditors, teachers—kindergarten and elementary, computer programmers, computer systems analysts—electronic data processing, electrical and electronic engineers, lawyers, physicians and surgeons, and mechanical engineers.

Information and data collected from BLS publications and other publications relative to the topic provide a fairly complete picture of manpower needs in the future. The ramifications of these needs vis a vis the higher education community can be discerned. The next step is to take a look at the distribution of blacks in higher education fields related to the identified needs.

Data Sources

Information and data for this paper were collected from a variety of sources. At the beginning stages, collection efforts were focused on productivity data. A great deal of effort was spent in getting data about program completers by fields of study by race. This effort was fairly fruitful for the middle and late nineteen seventies. As of this writing, it appears that there is a dearth of similar data for the nineteen eighties. Success has been

4

achieved, however, in finding data that indicate the intended field of study of blacks. Admittedly, major fields declared by freshman students undergo many changes before graduation four or five years later.

The largest source of data on the major fields and expected careers of students by race has been compiled from reports of the Cooperative Institutional Research Program (CIRP) administered by the University of California at Los Angeles in cooperation with the American Council on Education. Another major source of data was the U.S. Office of Education's Office of Educational Research and Improvement. Several items of data from these and other sources were provided by members of the NAFEO Research Institute Staff.

Discussion

The data shown in Table 1 address the nine high-growth occupations for college graduates projected for 1985–1990 by the U.S. Department of Labor, Bureau of Labor Statistics. Between 1984 and 1995, total employment has been projected by BLS to rise from 106.8 million to 122.8 million. The nine high-growth occupations shown in Table 1 are part of thirty-seven occupation that will comprise more than fifty percent of the job growth expected between 1984 and 1995. BLS expects that a college degree will either be required for employment in the nine occupations or will enhance prospects for applicants.

Accountants and Auditors. Employment for accountants and auditors is expected to expand by 307,000 from an estimated 882,000 in 1984, an increase of 35 percent. Employment opportunities in these occupations will in-

TABLE 1

Nine Projected High Growth Occupations in 1985–1995
for Which a College Degree Either Enhances
Employment Opportunity or is Required

Subgroup Occupation	Estimated Employment 1984*	Percent Change in Employment 1985–1995*	Numerical Change in Employment 1985–1995*
Executive, Administrative, and Managerial Occupations			
Accountants and Auditors	882,000	35	307,000
Engineers, Surveyors, and Architects			
Electrical and Electronic Engineers	390,000	53	206,000
Mechanical Engineers	237,000	34	81,000
Natural Scientists and Mathematicians			
Computer Systems Analysts	308,000	69	212,000
Social Scientists, Social Workers, Religious Workers and Lawyers			
Lawyers	490,000	36	174,000
Teachers, Counselors, Librarians, and Archivists			
Kindergarten and Elementary Teachers	1,381,000	20	281,000
Health Diagnosing and Treating Practitioners			
Physicians	476,000	23	109,000

Registered Nurses, *Pharmacists, Dietitians,* *Therapists, and* *Physicians Assistants*			
Registered Nurses	1,377,000	33	452,000
Technologists and *Technicians, Except* *Health*			
Computer Programmers	341,000	72	245,000

* = Estimates are from the BLS Industry-Occupation Matrix.
Source: U.S. Department of Labor, Bureau of Labor Statistics. *Statistical Abstract of the United States,* 1986.

crease much faster than average, according to BLS. Expectations are that college graduates will be in greater demand than applicants who lack college degrees.

Electrical and Electronics Engineers. The growing demand for computers, communication equipment and other electronic goods is expected to be the driving force behind the much faster than average expected increase in electrical and electronics engineering jobs. An expected growth rate of 53 percent is expected. One negative factor anticipated, however, for prospective college majors in these areas is the possibility of restrictions on enrollment due to shortages of faculty and laboratory equipment. The number of jobs is expected to grow from an estimated 390,000 in 1984 to 596,000 in 1995.

Mechanical Engineers. The estimated employment figure for mechanical engineers in 1984 was 237,000. This number is expected to grow by 81,000 in 1984–1995, an increase of 34 percent. The much faster than average increase is expected to come about as the result of growth in the demand for machinery and machinery

7

tools, as industrial machinery and processes increase in complexity.

Computer Systems Analysts. Employment in the occupation of computer systems analyst is expected to increase by an exceptionally high growth rate of 69 percent between 1984 and 1995. Two hundred and twelve thousand new workers will be added by 1995 to the 308,000 estimated for 1984. BLS expects that college graduates with courses in programming and systems analysis plus training and expertise in applied fields will have the best prospects for employment. The accelerated growth rate will parallel the increase in computer capabilities and the use of computers to solve a greater variety of problems.

Lawyers. Numerical change in employment for lawyers is expected to increase by 174,000 in 1984–1995. This change represents an increase of 36 percent. The faster than average growth rate is expected to be brought about by an increase in the need for legal services. According to BLS, prospects for establishing new practices will be best in small towns and expanding suburbs.

Kindergarten and Elementary School Teachers. Prospects for employment as a kindergarten or an elementary school teacher are expected to increase by 20 percent during 1984–1995. A total of 1,381,000 persons were employed in these areas in 1984. This figure is projected to grow by 281,000 during the years 1984–1995. Rising enrollments in kindergarten and elementary schools will improve the job market at a faster than average rate.

Physicians. The increasing health care needs of a growing and aging population is expected by BLS to accelerate the employment prospects for physicians. Change in employment figures is expected to increase by 109,000 above the 476,000 employed in 1984. Expectations are that the increase will consist largely of salaried

8

positions and that solo practitioners will continue to decline. The BLS expects that the substantial growth will increase competition and affect earnings. Prospects for employment will likely be best in large group practices, health maintenance organizations, clinics, and other out-patient facilities.

Registered Nurses. Employment opportunities for registered nurses is expected to grow by 452,000 during 1984–1995, an increase of 33 percent. Job prospects are expected to be especially favorable for nurses who have bachelor's degrees. The increased demand for nurses will be influenced mainly by health care needs of the growing and aging population. Other major growth factors for employment of registered nurses, according to BLS, include the complexity of hospital-based medical procedures and equipment; the rapid growth of health maintenance organizations, urgent care centers, surgicenters, corporate wellness centers, and other outpatient facilities.

Computer Programmers. The demand for computer programmers is expected to nearly double between 1984 and 1995. A growth rate of 72 percent is projected. This faster than average increase represents an increase of 245,000 new employment opportunities. A total of 341,000 persons were employed as computer programmers in 1984. The BLS expects that prospects for employment will be best for college graduates who major in computer and information science and have experience or training in fields such as accounting, management, engineering, or science.

Trends in Majors/Degrees

The fields of study chosen by black students will have a great impact on the opportunities for blacks to benefit from the 1984–1985 projected high growth occupations. The preferences of entering freshmen at all U.S. institutions and historically black colleges and universities (HBCUs) are shown in Table 2.

The relationship of majors indicated by freshmen to fields of study in which degrees are granted tend to vary. There is some evidence, however, that a substantive relationship exists between fields of study and subsequent career preferences.

Dramatic increases in preferences of majors did not occur among entering freshmen at HBCUs, except in the field of computer science. However, in reference to career preferences, the HBCU entering freshman consistently indicated a higher preference for becoming a lawyer or physician during the years shown in Table 2.

The average HBCU freshman with a major in accounting and nursing is generally higher than the national average for all institutions, whereas, the average HBCU freshman in engineering is slightly lower than the national average.

Degrees Conferred

The percentages of bachelor's degrees received by Blacks between 1975–1976 and 1984–1985 are shown in Table 3. These data represent data for the five most recent years that data were collected. The data shown do not relate directly to each high growth degree area because the degree data were aggregated by broad categories rather than by specific majors. The data shown in Table 3 do provide, however, an opportunity to examine outcomes in the fields of business and management, computer and information science, engineering, health professions, and law.

TABLE 2

Trends in Preferences for College Majors and Careers for Freshmen at All U.S. Institutions and at HBCUs

Major and Career Preference	Percent of Entering Freshmen Students by Year									
	1977		1979		1981		1983		1985	
	All	HBCUs	All	HBCUs	All	HBCUs	All	HBCUs	All	HBCUs
Major:										
Accounting	6.4	7.3	6.2	6.4	5.8	6.0	6.3	7.5	6.5	7.1
Elementary Education	2.6	3.9	2.2	3.2	2.6	1.9	2.4	1.9	3.2	2.9
Electrical or Electronic Engineering	3.2	2.4	3.2	3.7	3.6	2.5	4.3	2.9	3.9	3.3
Mechanical Engineering	1.8	1.2	2.0	.7	2.4	1.0	2.2	1.1	2.1	1.4
Nursing	4.4	4.2	3.6	3.4	3.8	6.2	4.4	2.3	3.3	6.1
Computer Science	1.0	.9	1.8	2.5	3.8	6.0	4.5	8.2	2.3	7.9
Career Preference:										
Lawyer	4.4	4.8	3.4	4.2	3.9	4.4	3.9	5.7	3.9	6.4
Physician	3.2	4.1	2.9	3.7	3.4	4.2	3.9	4.4	3.8	5.0

Note: The data represent weighted national norms

Source: *The American College Freshmen: National Norms for Fall, 1977, 1979, 1981, 1983, and 1985,* UCLA/ACE Cooperative Institutional Research Project.

TABLE 3

Bachelor's Degrees Awarded to Black Students by Discipline Division 1976, 1979, 1981, 1983, 1985

Discipline/ Division	1975–1976 Degrees Awarded	1975–1976 Percent of Total	1978–1979 Degrees Awarded	1978–1979 Percent of Total	1980–1981 Degrees Awarded	1980–1981 Percent of Total	1982–83 Degrees Awarded	1982–83 Percent of Total	1984–85 Degrees Awarded	1984–85 Percent of Total
Total	59,122	6.4	60,130	6.6	60,533	6.5	57,129	5.8	54,964	5.5
Agriculture and natural resources	267	1.4	346	1.5	380	1.7	364	1.7	347	2.0
Architecture and environmental design	259	2.8	316	3.4	300	3.2	334	3.4	324	3.5
Biological sciences	2,326	4.3	2,487	8.6	2,266	5.2	2,073	5.1	1,972	5.0
Business and management	9,489	6.7	11,430	6.6	13,388	6.7	13,777	6.0	14,172	6.0
Computer and information sciences	323	5.8	505	5.8	784	5.2	1,274	5.2	2,087	5.3
Education	14,209	9.2	11,509	9.1	9,494	8.8	6,826	6.8	5,221	5.8
Engineering	1,370	3.0	1,756	2.9	2,432	3.3	2,848	3.2	3,013	3.1
Health professions	2,741	5.1	3,380	5.4	3,603	5.7	3,774	5.8	3,704	5.6
Law	27	5.2	53	7.9	22	2.8	40	3.6	83	7.1
Mathematics	799	5.1	652	5.6	582	5.3	629	5.0	757	5.0
Physical sciences	647	3.0	691	3.0	886	3.8	839	3.6	803	3.4

Note: Figures for U.S. Outlying Areas are not included for 1976, 1979 and 1981.
Source: Office for Civil Rights (OCR), ED (Washington, 1976, 1979, 1981, 1983 and 1985), Unpublished Data.

More specific percentages of degrees awarded to blacks in medicine are shown in Table 4. The percentage of blacks graduating from medical school declined by three-tenths of a percent between 1975–1976 and 1980–1981. The absolute number of black medial school graduates, however, did increase. Eight hundred and twenty-eight blacks graduaed from medical school in 1984. This is an 11.4 percent increase over 1975.

The number of blacks graduating from law school in the years 1980 through 1984 is shown in Table 5. The data show that the percentage of blacks receiving law degrees, as compared to the total degrees awarded, was the same at the beginning and the end of this period. The percentage peaked at 4.5 percent in 1982. The number of blacks graduating from law school did increase during the period by 6.0 percent, from 1,461 in 1980 to 1,548 in 1984.

TABLE 4
Percentage of Black Americans Among the Medical School Graduates in the Years 1975 to 1984

Year	Black American Graduates	Total Graduates	Percent of Total
1975	743	13,634	5.4
1976	752	13,614	5.5
1977	791	14,391	5.5
1978	760	14,966	5.1
1979	768	15,135	5.1
1980	766	15,673	4.9
1981	763	15,985	4.8
1982	883	15,802	5.6
1983	818	16,343	5.0
1984	828	16,318	5.1

Source: Association of American Medical Colleges, 1986.

TABLE 5
Percentage of Black Americans Graduating from
Law School in the Years 1980–1984

Year	Black American Graduates	Total Law Graduates	Percent of Total
1980	1,461	35,059	4.2
1981	2,451	35,598	4.1
1982	1,563	34,846	4.5
1983	1,584	36,389	4.4
1984	1,548	36,687	4.2

Source: American Bar Association, 1985.

Employment of Blacks in High Growth Areas

The number of blacks employed in the nine projected high growth occupations during 1983–1985 increased slightly in each occupation, except that of physician. The percent of blacks in the two projected high growth areas of computer systems analysis and elementary school teachers has either declined or remained the same from 1983 to 1985. The picture for electrical and electronics engineers is not clear because of a change in the format for reporting engineering data (Table 6).

Conclusions

The survey of literature and data for this paper provided an overview of career opportunities for college graduates; career preferences, and majors selected by freshmen students; degrees awarded in the projected high growth occupation areas; and the employment status of

TABLE 6
Percent of Black Participation in Projected High Growth Occupations 1983–1985

Occupation	Total Employed (1,000)			Black Percent of Total		
	1983	1984	1985	1983	1984	1985
Accountants and Auditors	1,105	1,234	1,265	5.5	5.5	5.9
Electrical and Electronic Engineers	(1,572)*	(1,627)*	544	(5.8)*	(2.6)*	3.4
Mechanical Engineers			272			2.2
Computer Systems Analysts	276	310	359	6.2	5.3	5.5
Physicians	519	520	492	3.2	5.0	3.7
Registered Nurses	1,372	1,402	1,447	6.7	7.6	6.8
Lawyers and Judges	651	678	671	2.7	2.6	3.3
Computer Programmers	443	507	534	4.4	5.3	6.4
Elementary School Teachers	1,350	1,322	1,360	11.1	9.9	11.1

* = All engineers (data not provided by areas)
Source: U.S. Department of Labor, Bureau of Labor Statistics. *Statistical Abstract of the United States, 1987.*

15

blacks in the nine occupations projected by the U. S. Department of Labor, Bureau of Labor Statistics as high growth occupations for college graduates. The findings indicate that blacks are underrepresented in each of the projected high growth occupations in comparison to the percentage of blacks both in the total civilian labor force and in the total population of college students.

The fact that the nine projected high growth occupations will experience a more rapid increase combined with the fact that blacks are presently underrepresented in these high growth occupations signals a need to prepare blacks for employment in these areas.

Blacks have continued to increase in the number of college degrees attained in the high growth occupational areas; however, the percentage of blacks in comparison to other racial groups, continues to be much lower. The same is true for employment in the majority of the high growth occupations. A review of the data available clearly reveals a link between higher educational attainment and higher labor force participation in the projected high growth occupations for college graduates.

The twenty-first century will begin in just twelve years. Some writers say that we have already moved from an industrial society to an information society. The colleges and universities must become the catalysts for change in the next century. The great challenge to be faced will be to provide a work force trained to function effectively in the information society. As the literature indicates, jobs will become available; but there is a question as to whether the work force will possess the skills to fill them.

Charles E. Richard and Stephen Hawkins summed the career phenomenon up well in the spring 1986 issue of the *College Board Review* when they wrote:

"We are going to need an entirely new sophisticated, and highly trained work force. Higher education can make it happen! We must insure that our graduates have the capacity to learn, have fully developed analytical skills, are creative and critical thinkers, are able to utilize methods of inquiry, and can cope with demands of a society marked by extraordinarily rapid change . . ." P. 8

The higher education community must meet the challenge posed by the twenty-first century, and this must be done with a pursuit of excellence. The pursuit of excellence must be persistently conducted by careful planning and management. The future is not just something that we must go to. The future is something that must be influenced by planning. As John Naisbitt stated in his best seller, *Megatrends,* "While the shift from an agricultural to an industrial society took 100 years, the present restructuring from an industrial to an informational society took only two decades. Change is occurring so rapidly that there is no time to react; instead we must anticipate the future."

*The future of blacks in various fields of study provides a challenge for higher education leadership. The rapid change to be faced by higher education will require studying the present and looking to the future in order to prepare for the future.

*The modern educational sys. must provide an educational environment for blacks wherein they fell apart and not one that alienates and tolerates them.
a new and unique american leader will be the result of the past 10 - 15 years of our political history.

References

American Bar Association. *A Review of Legal Education in the United States*. Washington, D.C.: Fall, 1985.

Association of Medical Colleges. Fall Enrollment Survey, Washington, D.C., 1986.

Austin, William M., *The Job Outlook Brief,* (Occupational Outlook Quarterly, Volume 30, No. 2), Washington, D.C.: U.S. Government Printing Office, Spring 1986, pp. 3–9.

Baxter, Neal, *New Projections to 1995.* (Occupational Outlook Quarterly, Volume 30, No. 2), Washington, D.C.: U.S. Government Printing Office, Spring 1986, pp. 31–43.

Naisbitt, John, *Megatrends,* New York: Warner Books, Inc., 1984, p. 9.

Richard, Charles E. & Hawkins, S. *The Twenty First Century: Will Higher Education Prepare America? College Board Review,* Spring, 1986.

Sargent, Jon, *An Improving Job Market for College Graduates: The 1986 Update of Projections to 1995,* (Occupational Outlook Quarterly, Volume 30, No. 2), Washington, D.C.: U.S. Government Printing Office, Summer 1986, p. 3.

Sheppard, C. Stewart and Carroll, Donald C., *Working in the Twenty-First Century,* New York: John Wiley & Sons, 1980.

The American College Freshman: National Norms for fall, 1977, 1979, 1981, 1983 and 1985. UCLA/ACE Cooperative Institutional Reserve Project.

U.S. Department of Education, National Center for Educational Statistics. *Special Report, Participation of Black Students in Higher Education,* 1983.

Chapter II

Teacher Education:
Lost Ground for Blacks

Dr. Elaine P. Witty
Dean, School of Education
Norfolk State University, VA

this is one of the results of the Reagan Admin.

Black and other minority students are underrepresented in teacher education programs today. They are
also underrepresented in the teaching force. The declin-
ing percent of black high school graduates who go on to
college each year and the negative impact of teacher
testing and other educational reforms are combining to
create a crisis situation for teacher educators. The decrease in black and other minority teacher education
students and the decrease in the population of black and
other minority teachers are occurring at a time of increasing minority school age population. At the same
time there is turbulence in teacher education in general.

Black Representation in the Teaching Force

Currently, blacks constitute a smaller percent of the teachers in America than was the case six years ago. The Center for Education Statistics reported that 2,228,636 teachers were employed in public schools in Fall 1986 (Office of Educational Research and Improvement, 1987a). An alarmingly small percent of these teachers were black. The new National Education Association (NEA) survey revealed that in 1986, blacks comprised only 6.9 percent of the teaching force (NEA, 1987). This percent is down from 9.7 percent reported by the NEA in 1980 (NEA, 1980).

Black and other minority children are increasing in the public school enrollment. They account for nearly 30 percent of the elementary and secondary school-age population. Black students represent 16.2 percent of the children in public schools while black teachers represent only 6.9 percent of the teachers. For white teachers and white children, the situation is reversed. White children comprise 71.2 percent of the public school population, but white teachers comprise 89.6 percent of the teachers (Office of Educational Research and Improvement, 1987b and National Education Association, 1987).

Black Teacher Education Graduates

Data on the number of bachelor's degrees in education conferred to blacks and whites suggest that there is a continuing decline in the number of blacks who are available to apply for initial teaching certificates. Table 1 shows that in 1975–76 blacks received 14,229 degrees in education. This was 9.1 percent of the total degrees

TABLE 1

**Bachelor's Degrees Conferred to Blacks and Whites in Education by
All U.S. Institutions**

| Year | Total | GROUP | |
		Black	White
1975–76	156,538	14,229	135,514
1978–79	127,638	11,538	108,989
1980–81	110,715	9,517	93,750
1982–83	100,171	6,826	81,663
1984–85	90,511	5,221	74,918

Source: National Advisory Committee Staff Analysis, OCR Unpublished Data on Degrees Awarded by Major Field, Race/Ethnicity, and Sex—1975–76, 1976–77.

NAFEO Research Institute Staff Analysis of OCR Unpublished Data on Degree Awarded by Major Field, Race/Ethnicity, and Sex—1980–81, 1982–83, and 1984–85.

granted. In 1984–85, blacks received 5,221 degrees, only 5.8 percent of the degrees granted in education.

Black Teacher Education Enrollment

Prospects for improving black representation in the teaching force during the next few years are not encouraging. Minority teachers who will be available in the next one to four or five years should be enrolled in school today. However, a recent survey by the American Association of Colleges for Teacher Education (AACTE, 1987) revealed that in the 1271 colleges and universities that prepare teachers, blacks and other minority students represent a small present of the enrollment in programs leading to initial teacher certificates. The survey revealed that only 4.3 percent of the enrollees preparing to teach in elementary schools are black and only 4.1 percent of those preparing to teach in the secondary schools are black (AACTE, 1987).

Teaching as a career choice for college students has lost ground. A smaller percent of the college students majored in programs leading to teaching certificates in 1984–85 than in 1875–76. While education was the most frequently chosen field in 1975–76, it was the third most popular field in 1984–85. The number of baccalaureate degrees in education conferred to minority students dropped 50.2 percent from 1975–76 to 1984–85 (American Council on Education (ACE), 1987).

Black College-going Rate

Even though the percent and number of black high school graduates increased from 1976 to 1985, the college-going rate for blacks decreased during the same period. In 1976, 33.5 percent of the black high school graduates went on to college. In 1985, only 26.1 percent of high school graduates went to college. While there has been improvement in increasing the high school graduation rate from 3.3 million (67.5%) in 1976 to 3.7 million (75.6%) in 1985 (American Council on Education, 1987), there has been a loss to higher education and to teacher education in the number and percentage of blacks preparing for leadership roles in education.

Rather than joining the ranks of college students, many black high school graduates are selecting other options. Reports on the number of black high school graduates in post-secondary programs and activities indicate that a large percent of the non-college going black youth are joining the military or enrolling in proprietary business and technical schools. According to the ACE report, minorities make up a third of the Armed Forces and 40 percent of the enrollment in proprietary schools (American Council on Education, 1987).

Educational Pipeline Problem for Potential Black Teacher Education Students

There is a serious pipeline problem for black students. At each successive level of educational attainment, black participation declines. Blacks constitute 17 percent of elementary and secondary school enrollments, but represent only 10 percent of the college students, and receive only 7 percent of the bachelor's degrees awarded and 4 percent of the doctorates awarded (Office of Educational Research and Improvement, 1987).

Black school enrollment continues to fall short of the presence of blacks in the general population. U.S. Census data for 1980 indicate that blacks comprise 11.7 percent of the general population.

The increasing discrepancy between the percent of black and other minority teachers and the percent of black and other minority pupils may contribute to the problems of poor academic achievement for minority pupils and the subsequent reduction of the pool of black high school graduates and adequately prepared black college students. The shortage of minority mentors and advocates and the inaccessibility of adequate minority role models add to the difficulties minority children experience in school. Further, white pupils are denied the support and encouragement they may need to learn racial tolerance and respect for authority figures whose racial/ethnic backgrounds represent minority groups.

23

The College Board report, *Equality and Excellence: The Educational Status of Black Americans* (1985) indicates that the educational pipeline problems of black students may be related to disproportionate enrollment in special education programs, overrepresentation in vocational education programs and underrepresentation in academic programs and programs for the gifted and talented, inappropriate coursework selection in mathematics, physical sciences and social studies, and less access to microcomputers and programs leading to concept development. Problems such as these reduce the number of black students who are prepared for successful participation in teacher education programs. Even though the pool of black students entering kindergarten is adequate, the pool is reduced at various levels throughout the pipeline so that it is unacceptably small at the point of teacher education admission.

Financial considerations present other factors that influence black students' decisions about entering college and selecting teacher education for career preparation. Scholarships, loans and financial aid arrangements that help students afford rising tuition costs are inadequate to meet the need.

Impact of the Testing Movement

While teacher testing has been promoted as an important aspect of the efforts to improve education for public school students, one of its major effects has been to magnify the problem of black and other minority teacher decline. Without screening out an appreciable number of white teacher applicants, the tests have seriously reduced the number of black and other minority teacher applicants. In attempts to provide quality control to entrance into the teaching profession by 1990, 44 states will have mandatory tests for initial teacher certification and 27 states will have mandatory tests for admission into teacher education Programs (Office of Educational Research and Improvement, 1987c).

Whereas the stated purpose for starting the teacher testing movement was to prevent incompetent teacher education graduates from being awarded teacher certificates, states are now using testing to (1) admit students into teacher education programs, (2) evaluate teacher education programs, (3) screen candidates for initial certification, (4) provide an alternative to the approved program approach to certification, and/or (5) select teachers to participate in Master Teacher/Career Ladder programs.

Studies on the testing effects in ten states led Smith (1984) to report that "regardless of the state and regardless of the type of examination—entrance or exit, standardized or customized—disproportionate numbers of minority teachers are being screened out of the teaching profession." This finding is supported by reports by Dilworth (1986) and Weiss (1987).

The results reported by Cooper (1986) confirm the negative impact of testing on black teacher employment. Cooper's review of teacher statistics in ten southern states for the period 1980–81 to 1983–84, revealed that the number of black teachers has fallen by 6.4 percent while in the same period, the total number of teachers increased by 1 percent.

In order to combat the adverse impact of testing on teacher education programs, many historically black colleges and universities (HBCUs) have mounted extensive programs aimed specifically at improving student performance on teacher tests. Improvements have been reported at such institutions as Grambling (Joiner, 1985), the University of Arkansas at Pine Bluff (Pressman and Gartner, 1986), and Norfolk State University (Whitehurst, Wiggins, and Witty, 1986).

Impact of the Educational Reform Movement

Since 1983 when the Commission on Excellence issued *A Nation at Risk,* numerous reports proposing educational reforms have surfaced. Few of the suggested reforms are new, most have been tried and abandoned during earlier periods. Some of the reforms that are being adopted by state departments across the nation may excellerate the reduction of black and other minority teachers.

Proposals in the two publications—*A Nation Prepared: Teachers for the 21st Century* (Carnegie Forum on the Economy, 1986), and *Teachers for Tomorrow* (The Holmes Group, 1986)—call for an elimination of undergraduate degrees in education and the introduction of teacher preparation programs based in the undergraduate degree in arts and sciences with pedagogical preparation provided by a year of professional study after the bachelor's degree. The extended length of teacher education programs may serve as a disincentive that makes it more difficult to attract minorities into teacher education programs. For example, Garibaldi (1987) maintained that "the additional year of study and its comcomitant financial costs will discourage rather than entice black and white students from entering the profession as long as teaching salaries remain low" (p. 18). The cost of tuition and expenses for the extra year plus the additional cost

26

of not having a full time job for the extra year will present a financial handicap for many minority students. Faced with a choice of a longer teacher education program and other more attractive career possibilities, many minority students will, out of financial reasons, not choose teacher education.

Role of Historically Black Colleges and Universities in Teacher Education

Historically black colleges and universities (HBCUs) have been a source of a large percent of the current black teaching force. For example, Garbaldi (1986) reported that for the twenty-one colleges and universities in Louisiana, the state's five black universities produced 79 percent of the black teacher education graduates in 1976–77 and 67 percent in 1983. Many of these colleges are now facing challenges associated with low enrollment in teacher education programs and extraordinary efforts required to maintain an adequate student passing rate on the teacher tests.

In 1975–76, historically black colleges and universities (HBCUs) conferred 7,059 bachelor's degrees to black students and in 1984–85, the number had dwindled to 2,747 (National Advisory Committee Staff Analysis, 1978; NAFEO Research Institute, 1986). These data as well as the bachelor's degrees awarded in education by race/ethnicity are presented in Tables 2 and 3. The impact of this enrollment decline is illustrated by the studies conducted by Garibaldi (1986) which show that in Louisiana, the number of black teacher education graduates from the five historically black colleges and universities dropped from 745 in 1976–77 to 242 in 1982–83.

TABLE 2
Number and Percent Change of Bachelor's Degrees Awarded in
Education by Historically Black Colleges and Universities (HBCUs)
and All U.S. Institutions
1965–66 to 1984–88

Year	Total Degrees	Institution	
		HBCUs	**Non-HBCUs**
1965–66	118,399	7,065	111,334
1966–67	120,874	6,773	114,101
1967–68	135,848	6,914	128,934
1968–69	153,248	7,558	145,690
1969–70	166,423	8,197	158,226
1970–71	177,638	8,430	169,208
1975–76	156,538	7,420	149,118
1978–79	127,633	5,740	121,893
1980–81	110,715	3,691	107,024
1982–83	100,171	3,600	96,571
1984–85	90,511	2,747	87,764
Number and Percent Change			
1966–71	59,239	1,365	57,874
	(50.0)	(19.3)	(52.0)
1971–76	−21,100	−1,010	−20,090
	(−11.9)	(−12.0)	(−11.9)
1976–81	−45,823	−3,729	−42,094
	(−29.3)	(−50.3)	(−28.2)
1981–85	−20,204	−944	−19,260
	(−18.3)	(−25.6)	(−18.0)
1966–85	−27,888	−4,318	−23,570
	(−23.6)	(−61.1)	(−21.2)

Source: Degrees Geanted and Enrollment Trends in Historically Black Colleges: An Eight Year Study, Institute for Services to Education, 1974.
National Advisory Committee Staff Analysis, OCR Unpublished Data on Degrees Awarded by Major Field Race/Ethnicity, and Sex—1975–76, 1976–77, 1978–79.
NAFEO Research Institute Staff Analysis of OCR Unpublished Data on Degrees Awarded by Major Field, Race/Ethnicity, and Sex—1980–81, 1982–83, and 1984–85.

28

TABLE 3

Number of Bachelor's Degrees Awarded in Education by Historically Black Colleges and Universities (HBCUs) and All U.S. Institutions by Race/Ethnicity: 1976, 1979, 1981, 1983, and 1985

Year	No. of Insts. Awarding Degrees	Total Degrees	Black	Total Minority	White	N-R Alien	Balance*
1975–76							
Total	1,184	156,538	14,229	20,254	135,514	770	0
HBCUs	80	7,420	7,059	7,074	298	48	0
Non-HBCUs	1,104	149,118	7,170	13,180	135,216	722	0
1978–79							
Total	1,182	127,633	11,538	17,778	108,984	871	0
HBCUs	80	5,740	5,468	5,480	227	33	0
Non-HBCUs	1,102	121,893	6,070	12,298	108,767	838	0
1980–81							
Total	1,183	110,715	9,517	16,045	93,750	920	0
HBCUs	82	3,691	3,353	3,375	271	45	0
Non-HBCUs	1,101	107,024	6,164	12,670	93,479	875	0

29

1982–83							
Total	1,206	100,171	6,826	11,490	81,663	1,110	5,908
HBCUs	81	3,600	3,248	3,271	271	130	−72
Non-HBCUs	1,125	96,571	3,578	8,221	81,392	980	5,836
1984–85							
Total	1,206	90,511	5,221	9,383	74,918	968	5,232
HBCUs	80	2,747	2,190	2,216	242	134	155
Non-HBCUs	1,126	87,764	3,031	7,167	74,676	834	5,077

*Positive numbers indicate that racial distributions were not indicated. Negative numbers indicate that the racial distributions exceeded the total.

Source: National Advisory Committee Staff Analysis, OCR Unpublished Data on Degrees Awarded by Major Field Race/Ethnicity, and Sex—1975–76, 1976–77

NAFEO Research Institute Staff Analysis of OCR Unpublished Data on Degrees Awarded by Major Field. Race/Ethnicity, and Sex—1980–81, 1982–83, and 1984–85.

Recruitment Efforts for Black Teacher Education Students

Historically black colleges and universities (HBCUs) have intensified their recruitment efforts and expanded their reach to new audiences. A survey of selected HBCUs revealed that programs target junior high school students, high school seniors, college students in other fields, retired military persons, career switchers from business and industry, and paraprofessionals. These programs may be found in Kentucky State University, The University of Maryland—Eastern Shore Campus, Central State University, Hampton University, Tennessee State University, Virginia State University, North Carolina A. & T. State University, Jackson State University, Texas Southern University, and Norfolk State University (Witty, 1987).

An increasing number of traditionally white colleges and universities have initiated new recruitment and retention activities designed especially for minority students. Descriptions of sample programs were compiled by Holmes and Rosauer (1987). Programs included were identified according to the following sources of initiation: (1) institutions initiated, (2) institutional consortia, (3) state initiated, (4) local school district initiated, and (5) private foundation initiated. Although the programs described were focused on increasing minority participation in higher education in general, success of the programs will also increase the number of minority students in teacher education.

Since the 1982 publication of *Prospects for Black Teachers: Preparation, Certification and Employment* (Witty, 1982), a number of groups and professional organizations have addressed the issue of minority teacher recruitment and retention. The following descriptions include the major reports and the recommendations made.

National Commission for Excellence in Teacher Education of the American Association of Colleges for Teacher Education, *A Call for Change in Teacher Education,* 1985.
Recommends that federal and state governments, and private philanthropies, should ensure that the lack of finances will not bar qualified minority students from entering teacher education programs. Parents, teachers, counselors and principals should encourage minority students to consider careers in teaching; colleges and universities should provide a supportive climate; and above all, intellectually demanding teacher education programs should prepare graduates to meet certification requirements.

Task Force on the Future of Education of the American Federation of Teachers, 1986.
Recommends a four part approach to increasing the number of minority teachers: (1) Publicize issues of recruitment and retention of minority teachers as an area of shortage, (2) Mount programs at both high school and collegiate level to identify talented minority students who are potential teachers, strengthen their general school performance and prepare them adequately with emphasis upon overcoming test-taking obstacles, (3) Provide scholarships and loans at local, state and federal levels, with targeted funds designated for minorities, and (4) Target teacher recruitment and intern programs at institutions that attract significant numbers of minorities.

Holmes Group, *Tomorrow's Teachers,* 1986.
States that Holmes Group members should help to

create a profession representative of the larger society; proposes that members should: (1) increase recruitment at the precollege level, (2) endorse loan forgiveness programs for minority students entering teaching, (3) develop programs to increase retention of minority students, and (4) work to reduce the effects of handicapping conditions, poverty, race and ethnicity on the entry to the profession.

It should be noted that the Holmes Group propositions are aimed at member institutions only and that only one historically black institution (Howard University) was invited to membership.

Carnegie Forum on Education and the Economy, Task Force on Teaching as a Profession, *A Nation Prepared: Teachers for the 21st Century.*
Gives an excellent discussion on the rationale for providing a representative number of minority teachers and recommends the creation of a partnership of government, the private sector, the minority community and the schools to ensure an increasing number of minority teachers. The report points out that ''at the heart of the issue is the need to greatly increase the flow through the educational pipeline of members of these minority groups so they can join the pool of eligible candidates'' (p. 79).

Southern Regional Education Board. *SREB Recommendations to Improve Teacher Education,* 1986.
States that the number of minority teachers continue to decrease. Recommends (1) financial incentives to attract qualified minorities into teaching, and (2) extra efforts to insure that disadvantaged students who want to teach are prepared to meet the higher standards required for teachers.

Responding to the continuing decline in the number of black teacher education students enrolled in member institutions, the American Association of Colleges for Teacher Education released a policy statement on December 14, 1987. The statement, *Minority Teacher Recruitment and Retention: A Call for Action,* proposed ten specific programs: (1) National Scholarship Program, (2) State Scholarship Program, (3) Targeted High School Work-Study Program, (4) Targeted College Work-Study Program, (5) Two-Year/Four-Year Articulation Program, (6) Assistantships and Grants Program, (7) Entry Incentive Program, (8) Support Program for Reentry and Career Change, (9) Targeted Teacher Induction Program, and (10) Assessment Demonstration Grants Program. The AACTE announced its intentions to aggressively pursue programs and policies to assist member institutions to increase minority participation (AACTE, 1987).

It should be noted that the recommendations made by these groups have not been implemented; therefore, no evidence is available by which to gauge their impact on actually increasing the number of black and other minority teachers available for public schools.

Conclusions

Without significant intervention, black and other minority students will continue to represent a decreasing percent of the total teacher education student pool. The teaching force in America will become more white while the student population will become more non-white.

Encouraging intervention strategies have been proposed, however. Noteworthy are the efforts of historically black colleges and universities (HBCUs) that have devoted special resources to expand their recruitment and retention programs and to prepare students for the teacher tests.

Traditionally white universities are putting into operation numerous programs to recruit black college students and potential teacher education prospects. On a national level, professional organizations are gearing up to assist member institutions in recruiting and retaining black and other minority students.

Because of the complexity of the factors causing the problem, efforts at the colleges and universities will need to be supported by changes in educational policies. Educational reforms that reduce educational access should be studied to determine whether or not educational gain is commensurate to educational damage.

Improvements in the conditions surrounding teaching as a profession are also needed. Finally, closer networking among schools, communities, and colleges will help to increase the number of minorities, all along the educational pipeline, who will be available for teaching careers.

References

American Council on Education, Office of Minority Concerns. *Minorities in higher education* (Sixth annual status report). Washington, D.C.: American Council on Education, 1987.

American Association of Colleges for Teacher Education News Release, December 14, 1987. Washington, D.C.: American Association of Colleges for Teacher Education, 1987.

American Federation of Teachers Task Force on the Future of Education. *The revolution that is overdue*. New York: American Federation of Teachers, 1986.

Carnegie Forum on Education and the Economy, Task Force on

Teaching as a Profession. *A nation prepared: Teachers for the 21st century*. Washington, D.C.: Carnegie Forum, 1986.

Darling-Hammond, Linda. *Equality and excellence: the Educational Status of Black Americans*. New York: College Entrance Examination Board, 1985.

Cooper, C. Teacher testing and the vanishing Black teacher, Paper presented at the Seventh National Invitational Conference on Preparation and Survival of Black Public School Teachers, Norfolk State University, Norfolk, 1986.

Dilworth, Mary E. Teacher testing: adjustments for schools, colleges, and departments of education. *The Journal of Negro Education*, 1986, 55 (3) 368–378.

Garibaldi, A. M. *The decline of teacher production in Louisiana (1976–1983) and attitudes toward the profession*. Atlanta: Southern Education Foundation, 1986.

Garibaldi, Antoine M. Recruitment, admissions and standards: Black teachers and the Holmes and Carnegie Reports. *Metropolitan Education*, 1987 Spring (4), 17–23.

Holmes, Barbara J. and Ruth Rosaver. *General information relative to the recruitment and retention of minority teachers*. Denver, Colorado: Education Commission of the States, 1987.

Holmes Group. *Tomorrow's Teachers: A report of the Holmes group*. East Lansing, MI: The Holmes Group, Inc., 1986.

Joiner, Burnett. Grambling's efforts to increase test success rate 85 percent by Betty Cork. *The Advertiser*, August 16, 1985.

NAFEO Research Institute Staff Analysis of OCR Unpublished Data on Degrees Awarded by Major Field, Race/Ethnicity, and Sex 1980–81, 1982–83, and 1984–85.

National Advisory Committee Staff Analysis of OCR Unpublished Data on Degrees Awarded by Major Field, Race/Ethnicity, and Sex 1975–76 and 1976–77.

National Commission for Excellence in Teacher Education. *A call for change in teacher education*. Washington, D.C.: American Association for Colleges for Teacher Education, 1985.

National Education Association. *Status of the American public school teacher*, 1985–86; Washington, D.C.: National Education Association, 1987.

National Education Association. *Status of teachers and NEA members*. Washington, D.C.: National Education Association, 1980.

Office of Educational Research and Improvement, U.S. Department of Education. *E.D. TABS: Public School Enrollment and Staff, 1986–87*. Washington, D.C.: U.S. Department of Education, 1987a.

Office of Educational Research and Improvements, U.S. Department of Education. *Digest of educational statistics, 1987*. Washington, D.C.: U.S. Government Printing Office, 1987b.

Office of Educational Research and Improvement, U.S. Department of Education *What's happening in teacher testing; an analysis of state teacher testing practices*. Washington, D.C.: U.S. Government Printing Office, 1987c.

Pressman, H. and Gartner, A. The new racism in education. *Social Policy,* Summer, 1986.

Smith, G. Pritchy (Guest Editor): Equity and excellence in teacher assessment. *Urban Educator*. Detroit, MI: Wayne State University, Fall, 1986, 8(1).

Smith, G. Pritchy. Minority teaching force dwindles with state use of standardized tests: *AACTE Briefs,* 1984, 5(9) 12–14.

Southern Regional Education Board. *SREB Recommendations to Improve Teacher Education*. Atlanta, Georgia. Southern Regional Education Board, 1986.

Weiss, J. G. Testing teachers: strategies for damage control. In National Education Association, *What is the appropriate role of testing in the teaching profession?* Washington, D.C.: National Education Association, 1987.

Whitehurst, Winston, Witty, Elaine, & Wiggins, Samuel. Racial equity: teaching excellence, *Action in Teacher Education,* 1986, 8(1), 51–58.

Witty, Elaine P. Black teacher education pipeline and strategy survey. Unpublished report. Norfolk, Virginia: Norfolk State University, 1987.

Witty, Elaine P. *Prospects for black teachers: preparation, certification, employment*. Washington, D.C.: ERIC Clearinghouse on Teacher Education, 1982.

Chapter III

The Status of Black Americans in the Professions of Law and Medicine

Dr. Oscar L. Prater
V.P. for Administration
Hampton University, VA

Ms. Brendoler Miller
Research and Administrative Assistant
Hampton University, VA

The status of blacks in the professions of medicine and law is of increasing concern in the United States. This concern inspired this study which assesses the status of blacks in the professions of law and medicine in reference to population representation and other standards. Representation, as discussed in this chapter, refers to the level of parity between blacks as a percentage of these professions and blacks as a percentage of the general population. For example, in 1980, black Americans constituted 11.8 percent of the physicians and 4.2 percent of the practicing attorneys. Hence, a substantial increase of black Americans is needed in these professions to achieve parity with the population.

This study attempts to identify the existing supply of 1) black applicants to professional schools, 2) acceptees to professional schools, 3) first-year entrants to professional schools, 4) enrollees in professional schools, 5) graduates from professional schools, and 6) practitioners in law and medicine.

The study further identifies the supply necessary for parity with the population, the number of high school completions, and the number of students enrolled in colleges. Finally, the study compares the level of parity that presently exists with the levels for five and ten years earlier.

One overriding problem encountered is simply the lack of current, consistent and reliable data, particularly timely and accurate data on the number and characteristics of black practitioners in these professions. Most of the data considered in this report were provided by the law and medical associations. The latest data available were used in making the comparisons. The data elements which served as parity standards included data on the population, high school completion rates of 18 and 19 years old, and college enrollments of 18–24 years old.

Parity Standards

In this section, data on the population, high school completion, and college enrollments will be reviewed. These data elements will serve as parity standards. Whereas numerous other variables could have been selected for comparison purposes, the writers contend that

40

the ones selected are adequate for the purpose of this report.

Population

In 1985, 239,283,000 persons resided in the nation (Table I). Of this population, 29,012,000 or 12.1 percent were black Americans. Five and ten years earlier, the population of the nation was 227,738,000 and 215,973,000, respectively. Blacks comprised 11.8 percent of the population five years earlier and 11.5 percent ten years earlier. The 1985 population exceeded that of 1980 and 1975 by 5 percent and 10.8 percent, respectively. Black population as a percent of the total population in 1985 exceeded that of 1980 and 1975 by .3 percent and .6 percent. Both the total and black populations in 1985 exceeded that of 1980 and 1975. However, the rate of increase in the black population exceeded that for the total population, resulting in blacks comprising a greater percentage of the 1985 population than for either of the two earlier years discussed. In order for parity to exist for blacks in the professions of law and medicine, the percentage of blacks in these professions should be equal to their percentage of the population.

High School Completion

In 1975, of the 18 and 19 years old cohort, 4,992,000 students graduated from high school. Of this number, 476,000 or 9.5 percent were black (Table 2). The total number of graduates increased by 2.5 percent in 1980 and 4.0 percent in 1985 over that for 1975. The number

41

TABLE 1

Number and Percent of Blacks in the Total Population
1975–1985
(Numbers in Thousands)

Year	Total	Black Americans	Percent
1975	215,973	24,778	11.5
1976	218,036	25,157	11.5
1977	220,239	25,559	11.6
1978	222,585	25,984	11.7
1979	225,055	26,417	11.7
1980	227,738	26,905	11.8
1981	230,138	27,328	11.9
1982	232,520	27,759	11.9
1983	234,799	28,178	12.0
1984	237,019	28,594	12.1
1985	239,283	29,012	12.1

Source: U.S. Department of Commerce, Bureau of the Census. Current Population Reports, Series P-25, Nos. 310, 519, 917 and 1000.

of black graduates increased by 5.9 percent between 1980 and 1985 and 16.8 percent between 1975 and 1985. Blacks as a percent of the total number of graduates increased by .4 percent between 1980 and 1985 and 1.2 percent between 1975 and 1985.

Similar to population data, the number of graduates in 1985 exceeded that of 1980 and 1975 for both the total number of graduates and the number of black graduates. However, unlike the population data where steady increases in blacks as a percent of the total occurred annually, black graduates as a percent of all graduates fluctuated. Black graduates comprised a larger percentage of all graduates in 1985 than in 1980 and 1975. As with the population, efforts will be made to determine if parity exists for blacks when high school graduates are

TABLE 2
Number and Percent of Black Americans 18 and 19 Years Old Who
Have Completed Four Years of High School
1975–1985

Year	Total	Black Americans	Percent
1975	4,992,000	476,000	9.5
1976	5,181,000	515,000	9.9
1977	5,072,000	463,000	9.1
1978	5,019,000	482,000	9.6
1979	5,112,000	497,000	9.7
1980	5,116,000	525,000	10.3
1981	5,077,000	560,000	11.0
1982	5,005,000	589,000	11.8
1983	4,928,000	550,000	11.2
1984	4,714,000	566,000	12.0
1985	5,194,000	556,000	10.7

Source: U.S. Department of Commerce, Bureau of the Census, Current
Population Reports, *Educational Attainment in the United States,*
Series P-20, March 1985.

compared to professional practitioners and other status factors.

College Enrollment

Some 786,000 blacks were enrolled in college in 1984, 10.4 percent of the total college enrollment (Table 3). In 1980, 688,000 and in 1975, 665,000 black students were enrolled. Blacks comprised 9.7 percent and 8.2 percent of the total enrollments in 1980 and 1975, respectively. Blacks as a percentage of total enrollment in 1984 exceeded that of 1980 and 1975 by .9 percent and .8 percent, respectively (data were not available for 1985).

Blacks comprised a greater percentage of college enrollment in 1984 than in either of the other two years considered.

For each parity standard population, high school graduates, and college enrollment, the percentage of blacks at the present time as a component of the total exceeded that for the two earlier periods. For parity to exist when factors impacting the status of blacks in the professions are compared, a similar distribution must occur. Blacks as a percentage of practitioners in law and medicine in 1985 or the latest year which data were available should exceed that for 1980 and 1975.

Status Factors

The status factors to be considered in this report are applications to professional schools, acceptances to professional schools, entrants to professional schools, professional school enrollments, professional school graduates and practitioners in the profession.

TABLE 3

Black Americans as a Percent of Undergraduate College Enrollment
(Numbers in Thousands)

Year	Total	Black Americans	Percent
1975	6935	665	9.6
1980	7226	688	9.5
1981	7575	750	9.9
1982	7678	767	10.0
1983	7477	741	9.9
1984	7591	786	10.4

Source: Census Bureau, *U.S. Statistical Abstracts* (1981, 1982–83, 1984, 1985, 1986).

In this section of the report, data on each status factor will be reviewed. The latest year's data will be compared with data for 1980 and 1975, which in most cases will reflect periods of time five and ten years earlier. The resulting information will be compared with the parity standards, population, high school graduates, and undergraduate college enrollment.

Applications to Professional Schools

The data appropriate for this report on the number of applications from blacks to law school were not available for the years prior to 1980. Table 4 contains the information on all law school applicants.

The number of applications by blacks in 1985 was 4852, constituting an increase of 3.5 percent from 1980. The total number of applicants decreased 8.2 percent between 1980 and 1985, indicating a general loss of interest for non-black applicants.

When a comparison of black law applicants as a per-

TABLE 4

Black Americans as a Percent of all Applicants to Law School

Year	Total	Black Americans	Percent
1980	70,999	4,687	6.6
1981	72,911	4,711	6.5
1982	71,755	4,904	6.0
1983	64,100	4,591	7.2
1984	63,338	4,406	7.0
1985	65,210	4,852	7.4

Source: Law School Admissions Council (unpublished data), 1986.

centage of all law school applicants was made with that for blacks as a percentage of the population, the black population in 1980 exceeded the percent of applicants by 5.2 percent and 4.7 percent in 1985. Thus an increase in the level of parity existed during the five year time period.

In 1980, blacks as a percentage of the number of high school completions exceeded that percent of blacks as a percentage of law applicants by 3.7. An increase in the level of parity occurred over the 5 year period.

Blacks as a percent of college enrollment exceeded that of applicants to law school in 1980 by 3.1 percent and 3.4 percent in 1984. The decreased level of parity between college enrollment and the number of applicants for 1980 and 1984 is similar to the decrease in the level of parity levels experienced when the black applicants are compared to high school completions.

Applications to professional schools reflect the level of interest in pursuing careers in the professions. The percentage of black applicants in relationship to the total number of applicants to medical school was less than the percentage of blacks in the population, high school completions and college enrollment for 1975, 1980 and 1985. Hence, black applicants are underrepresented when compared to each parity standard.

As can be observed in Table 5, the number of applications to medical school by blacks in 1985 was 2428, constituting a decrease of 6.4 percent from the number in 1980 and an increase of 6.1 percent over the number in 1975, hence indicating an increase in interest between 1975 and 1985 and a decrease between 1980 and 1985. The total number of applications to medical school decreased 22.2 percent between 1975 and 1985 and 8.9 percent between 1980 and 1985, indicating a general loss

of interest as a group. Blacks as a percent of all applicants in 1985 exceeded that of 1980 by .2 percent and
that of 1975 by 2.0 percent. Blacks applicants comprised
a larger percentage of the total number of applicants in
1985 than in 1980 and 1975.

In 1975, blacks as a percent of the population exceeded
blacks as a percent of the number of applicants by 6.1
percent, in 1980 by 4.6 percent and in 1985 by 4.7
percent. Hence, a lower level of parity existed between
blacks as percentages of the population and applicants in
1985 than in 1980 but at a higher level than in 1975.

When comparisons of black applicants as a percentage
of the total were made with blacks as a percentage of the
number of high school completions, in 1975 the percent
of completions exceeded the percent of applicants by 4.1
percent, 3.1 percent in 1980 and 3.3 percent in 1985. The
level of parity between blacks as applicants and as high

TABLE 5

Black Americans as a Percent of all Applicants to Medical School

Year	Total	Black Americans	Percent
1975	42,303	2288	5.4
1976	42,155	2523	6.0
1977	40,557	2487	6.1
1978	36,636	2564	7.0
1979	36,141	2599	7.2
1980	36,100	2594	7.2
1981	36,727	2644	7.2
1982	35,730	2600	7.3
1983	35,200	2558	7.3
1984	35,944	2620	7.3
1985	32,893	2428	7.4

Source: Association of American Medical Colleges, 1986.

school completions was higher in 1985 than in 1980 but lower than 1975.

Blacks as a percent of college enrollment exceeded that of applicants to medical school in 1975 by 2.8 percent, in 1980 by 2.5 percent and in 1984 by 3.1 percent. Similar to the previous comparison, a higher level of parity existed between blacks as a percentage of college enrollment and as applicants in 1975 and in 1980 than in 1984.

Acceptees to Professional School

Information on the number of black acceptees to law school was not available. Table 6 contains the information on medical school acceptees.

Nine hundred and ninety-three (993) black Americans

TABLE 6

Black Americans as a Percent of All Acceptees to Medical School

Year	Total	Black Americans	Percent
1975	15,365	945	6.2
1976	15,774	966	6.1
1977	15,977	966	6.0
1978	16,527	970	5.9
1979	16,886	1024	6.1
1980	17,146	1057	6.2
1981	17,286	1037	6.0
1982	17,294	1001	5.8
1983	17,209	1019	5.9
1984	17,194	1049	5.8
1985	17,228	993	5.8

Source: Association of American Medical Colleges, 1986.

were accepted to medical school in 1985. This group constituted 5.8 percent of all acceptees to medical school for this year. The total number of acceptees for this year exceeded that for both the five and ten year earlier periods. This was not the case for black acceptees. The number of black acceptees in 1985 was less than that for 1980 but exceeded that for 1975. The decrease in acceptees between 1980 and 1985 was 6.1 percent and the increase between 1975 and 1985 was 5.1 percent.

Blacks constituted 6.2 percent of all acceptees in 1975 and 1980 but only 5.8 percent of the acceptees in 1985. Blacks as a percentage of the population exceeded blacks as a percentage of acceptees in 1975 by 5.3 percent, by 5.6 percent in 1980 and by 6.3 percent in 1985. A lower degree of parity existed with the population in 1985 than it did in either 1980 or 1975. The same was true when the level of black acceptees was compared with high school graduates and college enrollees.

A comparison was made between black and non-black applicants to medical school for the years 1975, 1980 and 1985. This information is shown in Table 7.

For the three years, 1975, 1980, and 1985, the number of black applicants remained about the same: 2288, 2594, and 2428, but substantial decreases were encountered with non-black applicants: 40,015, 33,506 and 30,465. The percent of black applicants accepted for the three years was 41.3 percent, 40.7 percent and 40.9 percent compared to 36.0 percent 48.0 percent and 53.3 percent for non-blacks.

Whereas a relatively close level of parity existed between blacks and non-black acceptees as a percent of applicants in 1975, ten years later in 1985, black acceptees dropped some 12.4 percent below the level of non-blacks.

49

TABLE 7

Acceptees as a Percent of Medical School Applicants
(Black and Non-Black Americans)

Year	Blacks Accepted	Blacks Applied	Percent	Non-Blacks Accepted	Non-Blacks Applied	Percent
1975	945	2,288	41.3	14,420	40,015	36.0
1976	966	2,523	38.3	14,808	39,632	37.4
1977	966	2,487	38.8	15,011	38,070	39.7
1978	970	2,564	37.8	15,557	34,072	45.7
1979	1,024	2,599	39.4	15,862	33,542	47.3
1980	1,057	2,594	40.7	16,089	33,506	48.0
1981	1,037	2,644	39.2	16,249	34,083	47.7
1982	1,001	2,600	38.5	16,293	33,130	49.2
1983	1,019	2,558	38.0	16,190	32,642	49.6
1984	1,049	2,620	40.0	16,145	33,324	48.4
1985	993	2,428	40.9	16,235	30,465	53.3

Source: Association of American Medical Colleges, 1986.

First Year Entrants

The number of black American first year entrants to medical school in 1985 exceeded that of 1975 by 11.3 percent and 1980 by 1.3 percent. The number of total first year entrants in 1985 exceeded that for 1975 by 10 percent and 1980 by .6 percent (Table 8).

The level of parity between first year entrants to medical school as it relates to blacks was less in 1985 than it was in 1980 and 1975 when compared to the population, high school completions and college enrollments. The level of parity in 1985 was .5 percent less than that in 1975 and .2 percent when considering the population; 1.1 percent and 2.2 percent for high school completions and 2.1 percent and .6 percent for college enrollment. The number of first year entrants of blacks to medical school was less representative in 1985 than ten years earlier

TABLE 8

Black Americans as a Percent of All First Year Entrants to Medical School

Year	Total	Black Americans	Percent
1975	14,910	893	6.0
1976	15,282	935	6.1
1977	15,493	959	6.2
1979	16,054	938	5.8
1980	16,301	981	6.0
1981	16,590	1,013	6.1
1982	16,644	1,001	6.0
1983	16,567	961	5.8
1984	16,480	992	6.0
1985	16,395	994	6.1

Source: Association of American Medical Colleges, 1986.

when population, high school completions, and college enrollment were considered.

When first year entrants to law school were considered, the picture differed slightly from that of medical school. Blacks as first year entrants comprised a larger percentage of all first year entrants in 1985 than it did in 1980 and 1975. A larger number of blacks entered law school in 1985 than during the other two periods. The total number of entrants in 1985 exceeded that for 1975 but was less than that for 1980 (Table 9).

The number of black entrants in 1985 exceeded those for 1980 by 1.8 percent where as the total number of entrants in 1985 was 3.5 percent less than in 1980.

When compared with the population, the level of parity between first year entrants in 1985 and 1980 was the same, but both were less than that for 1975. When compared to high school completions, the 1985 level was

TABLE 9
Black Americans as a Percent of First Year Entrants to Law School

Year	Total	Black Americans	Percent
1975	39,038	2,045	5.2
1976	39,996	2,128	5.3
1077	39,676	1,945	4.9
1978	40,479	2,021	5.0
1979	40,717	2,002	4.9
1980	42,296	2,144	5.1
1981	42,521	2,238	5.3
1982	42,034	2,217	5.3
1983	41,159	2,247	5.5
1984	40,747	2,214	5.4
1985	40,796	2,183	5.4

Source: American Bar Association, 1985.

lower than 1980 and 1975, with the same being true for college enrollment.

The level of parity of blacks as first year entrants to law schools in 1985 was equal to that of 1980 but less than that of 1975 when compared to the population and less than that for two other periods when compared to high school completions and college enrollment.

Professional School Enrollment

The total enrollment, as well as black enrollment, for medical school in 1985 exceeded that of 1980 and 1975 (Table 10).

Black enrollment in medical schools in 1985 exceeded 1980 by 3.8 percent and 1975 by 11.4 percent. In 1985, the total enrollment in medical school exceeded that of

TABLE 10

Black Americans as a Percent of Enrollment in Medical School

Year	Total	Black Americans	Percent
1975	55,818	3,456	6.2
1976	57,765	3,517	6.0
1977	60,039	3,587	6.0
1978	62,213	3,537	5.7
1979	63,800	3,627	5.7
1980	65,189	3,708	5.7
1981	66,298	3,884	5.9
1982	66,748	3,869	5.8
1983	67,327	3,892	5.8
1984	67,016	3,944	5.9
1985	66,585	3,849	5.8

Source: Association of American Medical Colleges, 1985.

1980 by 2.1 percent and 1975 by 19.3 percent. Blacks as a percentage of total enrollment in 1985 exceeded that of 1980 by .1 percent but was less than that of 1975 by .4 percent.

The level of parity for black enrollment in medical school in 1985 was lower than 1980 and 1975 when compared with the population, high school completions and college enrollments. The enrollment of blacks in medical school was less representative in 1985 than it was five and ten years earlier.

The enrollment of blacks in law school in 1985 exceeded that of 1980 and 1975, whereas the total enrollment in law school exceeded that for 1975 but was less than that for 1980 (Table 11).

Blacks as a percent of total law school enrollment was 4.9 percent in 1985, 4.4 percent in 1980 and 4.4 percent in 1975.

TABLE 11

Black Americans as a Percent of Enrollment in Law Schools

Year	Total	Black Americans	Percent
1975	116,991	5,127	4.4
1976	117,451	5,503	4.7
1977	118,557	5,304	4.5
1978	121,606	5,350	4.4
1979	122,860	5,257	4.3
1980	125,397	5,506	4.4
1981	127,312	5,789	4.5
1982	127,828	5,852	4.6
1983	127,195	5,967	4.7
1984	125,698	5,955	4.7
1985	124,092	6,051	4.9

Source: American Bar Association, 1985.

Though blacks comprised a larger percentage of the enrollment in 1985 than the other two years, it had little impact as it relates to parity with the standards. To reach parity with the population in 1985, black enrollment needed to increase 7.2 percent, 7.4 percent in 1980, and 7.1 percent in 1975. Hence, the level of parity with the population was higher in 1985 than in 1980 but lower than in 1975. A similar picture resulted when comparison was made with high school completions. Black enrollment needed to increase 5.8 percent for parity in 1985, 5.9 percent in 1980 and 5.1 percent in 1975. When it is compared to the college enrollment, a lower level of parity existed in 1985 than for the previous two periods examined. Some 5.5 percent was needed for parity in 1985, 5.3 percent in 1980 and 3.8 percent in 1975.

Graduates (Professional Schools)

The number of black graduates from medical school in 1984 exceeded that of 1980 and 1975 by 8.1 percent and 11.4 percent, respectively. The total number of graduates in 1985 exceeded those in 1980 by 4.1 percent and in 1975 by 19.7 percent. The largest number of black graduates occurred in 1982; however, the largest number of graduates occurred in 1983 (Table 12).

Blacks as a percent of all graduates in 1985 exceeded that of 1980 but was less in 1975.

The level of parity between graduates from medical school in 1985 and the population as it relates to blacks was .9 percent less than the level in 1975 but was only .1 percent less than the level for 1980. However, when compared with high school completions, the 1985 level was .2 percent less than that for 1980 and 1.5 percent less than 1975. A similar picture was reflected when comparison was made with college enrollment. The 1985 level was 2.6 percent less than 1975 and .7 percent less than 1980. Blacks were less representative on each parity standard as graduates from medical school in 1985 than they were in 1980 and 1975.

The number of blacks graduating from law school in 1984 was 6.0 percent more than in 1980 (Table 13).

TABLE 12

Black Americans as Percent of All Graduates from Medical Schools

Year	Total	Black Americans	Percent
1975	13,634	743	5.4
1976	13,614	752	5.5
1977	14,391	791	5.5
1978	14,966	760	5.1
1979	15,135	768	5.1
1980	15,673	766	4.9
1981	15,985	763	4.8
1982	15,802	883	5.6
1983	16,343	818	5.0
1984	16,318	828	5.1

Source: Association of American Medical Colleges, 1986.

TABLE 13

Black Americans as a Percent of Law School Graduates

Year	Total	Black Americans	Percent
1980	35,059	1,461	4.2
1981	35,598	1,451	4.1
1982	34,846	1,563	4.5
1983	36,389	1,584	4.4
1984	36,687	1,548	4.2

Source: American Bar Association, 1985.

The total number of graduates in 1984 exceeded that of 1980 by 4.5 percent. There was no change in the number of blacks as a percent of all graduates between these years: blacks comprised 4.2 percent of the total number. Black graduates from law school fell short as a representative group for each parity standard group. In 1984, 7.9 percent, 6.5 percent and 6.2 percent increases in the number of black graduates were needed to reach a level of parity with the population, high school completions and college enrollment, respectively.

Practitioners

Data relative to the number of practicing physicians can be observed in Table 14. The number of practicing black physicians in 1985 exceeded that of 1980 by 32.8 percent, whereas the total number of physicians increased by 11.3 percent for the same years. Hence, the greater increase in the number or black physicians resulted in blacks comprising a larger percentage of the

TABLE 14
Black Americans as a Percent of Practicing Physicians

Year	Total	Black Americans	Percent
1980	467,700	11,745	2.5
1981	478,300	12,516	2.6
1982	144,900	13,287	2.7
1983	499,500	14,058	2.8
1984	510,100	14,829	2.9
1985	520,700	15,600	3.0

Source: Bureau of Health Professions (unpublished data), 1986.

total group in 1985 than in 1980. The increase in this percentage was .5 percent.

A 9.1 percent increase in the number of black practicing physicians in 1985 was needed to bring the physicians up to parity with the population. A 9.6 percent increase was needed in 1980. Hence, a higher level of parity in 1985 existed than did in 1980 when the population is used as the parity standard. A similr result occurred when comparison was made with the high school completions. A 7.7 percent increase in the number of black physicians is needed for parity with high school completions in 1985 with 7.8 percent needed in 1980. In 1980, black physicians were 7.2 percent below parity wheres in 1985 they were 7.4 percent below parity.

There were 18.9 percent more black lawyers than black physicians in 1984. The total number of attorneys in 1985 exceeded the number in 1980. Hence, black lawyers as a percent of all lawyers increased between 1980 and 1985 (See Table 15).

When compared with the population, a 9.5 percent increase in black attorneys is needed in 1985 to generate parity.

The same was true when comparisons were made with high school completions and college enrollments. Between 1980 and 1985 the level of parity dropped 2.0 percent and .3 percent for high school completions and college enrollments, respectively.

Data Assessment

Parity Standards

Population

In 1985, 12.1 percent of the nation's population consisted of black Americans. This percent exceeded that

TABLE 15
Blacks as a Percent of Practicing Lawyers

Year	Total	Black Americans	Percent
1980	530,000	15,000	2.8
1981	581,000	*16,443	2.8
1982	630,000	18,270	2.9
1983	651,000	17,577	2.7
1984	678,000	17,628	2.6
1985	671,000	22,143	3.3

*In 1981, black Americans were not disaggregated from other minorities; therefore, a ratio proportion formula was used to estimate the number of black Americans in the total number of 26,726 which included blacks and other minorities.

$$\frac{15,000}{530,000} = \frac{x}{581,000} = 16,443$$

Source: Census Bureau, *U.S. Statistical Abstract* (1981, 1982–83, 1984, 1985, 1986).

for blacks as a component of the population in both 1980 and 1975, despite the fact that the nation's population in 1985 exceeded that of 1980 and 1975 by 5 and 10.8 percent, respectively. The change in the black population for the years considered was greater than that for the nation as a whole.

High School Completions

In 1975, of the 18 and 19 years old cohort, 4,992,000 students completed high school. Of this number, 476,000 or 9.5 percent were black Americans. Blacks comprised 10.3 percent of the graduates in 1980 and 10.7 percent in 1985. Though all graduates as well as black graduates increased over the years, black graduates increased at a faster pace than the total group.

College Enrollment

In 1984, the latest year data were available, 786,000 blacks were enrolled in college, comprising 10.4 percent of the total college enrollment. In 1980 and 1975, blacks comprised 9.7 percent and 8.2 percent, respectively. As with the other two standards, blacks as a percentage of the total in 1985 exceeded that for each of the prior periods. However, when we look at the total number of blacks in all age groups, we find that between 1976–1980 there was a 5 percent increase, whereas from 1980–1984 there was a 3.8 percent decrease.

Status of Professions

Medicine

As a percent of those interested in medicine, blacks constituted a larger percentage in 1985 than in 1980 or 1975. This resulted from the substantial drop in the total number of persons applying to medical school in 1985. The total number of applicants decreased from about 42,000 in 1975 to about 33,000 in 1985, whereas the number of black applicants remained about the same. Only 5 more applications were submitted by blacks in 1985 than were submitted 10 years earlier.

Despite the increase in interest by blacks as a percentage of the total, the number judged qualified to attend medical school, as a percent of the total, declined. Blacks comprised a smaller percentage of those accepted in 1985 than in 1980 or 1975. Considering acceptance rates as a percent of the applicants, the rates for blacks were 41.3 percent, 40.7 percent and 40.9 percent, respectively. However, for non-blacks, the rates were 36.0 percent, 48.0 percent and 53.3 percent.

First year entrants reflected about the same picture for blacks as the acceptances. Blacks as a percent of all first year entrants in 1985 comprised a smaller percentage than in 1980 or 1975. Blacks as a percent of the total enrollment in undergraduate colleges exceeded that 5 years earlier, but was less than that 10 years earlier. In 1974, blacks constituted 6.2 percent of all college enrollment, but only 5.8 percent in 1985. However, blacks enrolled in college did increase 11.4 percent between these two years.

The graduation rates for blacks were similar to those for the enrollment. Blacks as a percent of the total number of graduates in 1985 exceeded that for 1980 but was less than 1975. The number of blacks graduating from medical school increased 11.4 percent between 1975 and 1985.

As a percent of the total number of practicing physicians, blacks had a higher percentage in 1985 than in 1980. Data were not available for 1975. The number of black doctors increased 32.8 percent between 1980 and 1985, compared to 11.3 percent for all doctors for the same time period.

Relative to the totals in the field, blacks occupy a lower position in 1985 than 5 years earlier in the acceptance to and first year entrants into medical school, graduation from medical school and serving as practicing physicians. When compared with ten years earlier blacks occupy a lower position in acceptance to medical school, first year entrance to medical school, enrollment in medical school, and graduation from medical school. The improved position is the number of applicants. No information on practitioners was available for 10 years earlier. Table 16 contains a summary of blacks as percentage of the total for each factor measured.

TABLE 16

Medicine
Blacks as a Percent of Totals
(Impacting Factors)

Factor	Year		
	1975	1980	1985
Applicants	5.4	7.2	7.4
Acceptees	6.2	6.2	5.8
First Year	6.0	6.0	6.1
Enrollment	6.2	5.7	5.8
Graduates	5.4	4.9	5.1
Practitioners	—	2.5	3.0

The major measurement of the status of blacks will be in terms of the levels of parity that exist between impacting factors and the population, high school completions and undergraduate enrollment. In 1985, the number of applicants to medical school needed to increase 4.7 percent in order to be on par with the population. An increase of 4.6 percent was needed in 1980, and 6.1 percent in 1975. In terms of applicants and the population, blacks today reflect a higher level of parity than in 1975, but a lower level than in 1980. The same picture was reflected when comparisons were made with high school completions. The level of parity of black applicants today was lower when compared to college enrollment in both 1980 and 1975 (Table 17).

When comparisons are made between acceptances and the population, high school completions and college enrollment, a lower level of parity existed in 1985 than for either 1980 or 1975 for all three areas.

Blacks as first year entrants to medical school had a higher level of parity in 1985 when compared to the

62

TABLE 17
Medical Profession
Parity Levels
(Blacks as a Percent of Total)

| | Standards | | |
Factor	Population	High School Completions	College Enrollment
Applicants			
1975	6.1	4.1	2.8
1980	4.6	3.1	2.5
1985	4.7	3.3	3.1*
Acceptees			
1975	5.3	3.3	2.0
1980	5.6	4.1	3.5
1985	6.3	4.9	4.6
First Year Entrants			
1975	5.5	3.5	2.2
1980	5.8	4.3	3.7
1985	6.0	4.6	4.4
Enrollment Professional School			
1975	5.3	3.3	2.0
1980	6.1	4.6	4.0
1985	6.3	4.9	4.6
Graduates			
1975	6.1	4.1	2.8
1980	6.9	5.4	4.8
1985	7.0	6.9	5.3
Practitioners			
1975	—	—	—
1980	9.3	7.8	7.2
1985	9.1	7.7	7.4

*1984 data were used

63

population than in 1980 and 1985. A lower level of parity existed when compared to high school completions and college enrollment.

Considering enrollment in professional school in terms of parity, 1985 had a lower level of parity than both 1980, and 1975. The same was true for the professional school graduates.

Blacks as physicians were more representative of the population and high school completions in 1985, than they were in 1980. They had a lower level of parity in 1985 than 1980 when compared to college enrollment.

Law

Table 18 contains a summary of blacks as a percentage of the totals for each factor measured.

As a percent of the number of first year entrants to law school, blacks comprised a larger percentage in 1985 than in 1980 and 1975. Consistently, the total number of black entrants in 1985 exceeded the number entering in

TABLE 18
Law
Blacks as a Percent of Totals
(Impacting Factors)

Factor	Year		
	1975	1980	1985
Applicants	—	—	7.4
Acceptees	—	—	—
First Year Entrants	5.2	5.1	5.4
Enrollment Medical School	4.4	4.4	4.9
Graduates	—	4.2	*4.2
Practitioners	—	4.2	*2.6

*1984 data were used

64

1980 and 1975. The same was also true for the total number of first year entrants. A greater number of first year entrants existed in 1985 than in 1980.

A similar picture was presented when law school enrollments were considered. Blacks as a percentage of the total enrollment was greater in 1985 than in 1980 and 1975.

Information on black graduates from law schools in 1975 was not available. Blacks comprised approximately 4.2 percent of all graduates in both 1980 and 1985.

Practicing black lawyers comprised a smaller percentage of all lawyers in 1984 than in 1980 and 1977. Between 1977 and 1984, the number of black lawyers increased 19.2 percent and decreased 30.3 percent between 1980 and 1984. This substantial decrease accounted for the low percentage of the total in 1984.

Relative to the totals in the law profession, blacks occupied a more favorable position in 1985 than they did five years earlier in the number of first year entrants and enrollments and an equal position in the number of graduates. The only unfavorable position was the number of practitioners. (Table 19)

In 1985, blacks as first year entrants to law school needed to increase 6.7 percent to achieve parity with the population and in 1980, 6.7 percent was needed. In 1975, 6.3 percent was needed. A higher level of parity existed between the first year entrants and the population in 1985 than in 1975, but was the same as 1980. The same was not the case when compared with high school completions and college enrollment. A lower level of parity existed in 1985 than in either 1980 or 1975 for both of these standards.

Considering the parity status for medical enrollment, a higher level existed in 1985 than in 1980 when com-

TABLE 19
Law Profession
Parity Levels
(Blacks as a Percent of Total)

Factor	Population	Standards High School Completions	College Enrollment
Applicants			
1975	—	—	—
1980	5.2	3.7	3.1
1985	4.7	3.3	3.4*
First Year Entrants			
1975	6.3	4.3	3.1
1980	6.7	5.2	4.5
1985	6.7	5.3	5.0
Enrollment			
Professional School			
1975	7.1	5.1	3.8
1980	7.4	5.9	5.3
1985	7.3	5.8	5.5
Graduates			
1975	—	—	—
1980	7.6	6.1	5.5
1985	7.9	6.5	6.2
Practitioners			
1975	—	—	—
1980	7.6	6.1	5.5
1985	9.5	8.1	7.8

*1984 data were used

pared with the population, but a lower level than 1975. The same was true when the comparison was made with high school completions. A lower level existed in 1985 than in 1980 and 1975 when medical school and high school enrollments were compared.

A higher level of parity existed in 1980 than in 1984 when graduates were compared with the population, high school completions and college enrollment. No data was available for years prior to 1980. The same picture was reflected when practitioners were compared.

Summary and Conclusions

The strategy in undertaking this project was to identify several standards and compare relevant factors impacting the status of blacks in these professions with the standards. The underlying assumption being that black Americans as participants in these professions should be representative of the standards selected. The standards selected are referred to as parity standards for purposes of this study.

The parity standards selected were the population of the nation, the number of high school completions and enrollment in undergraduate colleges. These three variables were selected because of their importance as prerequisites to pursuing the medical and law professions.

Impacting factors on the status of blacks in these professions were identified as:

• Interest in pursuing these professions as determined by the number of applications to professional schools
• Qualification to attend professional schools as determined by the number of acceptees
• Initiative to pursue these professions as determined by the number of first year entrants
• Enrollment in professional schools
• Graduation from professional schools
• The number or percentage of practicing professionals

The status of the professions was determined as a result of comparing the level of parity that existed between the impacting factors and the standards for 1985, 1980 and 1975. The objective was to determine if the status of these professions was more or less favorable in 1985 than it was five and ten years earlier.

In 1985, 12.1 percent of the nation's population consisted of black Americans. This percent exceeded that for black Americans as a component of the population in both 1980 and 1975, wherein blacks constituted 11.8 percent and 11.5 percent of the population, respectively. In order to reflect parity with the population, a similar distribution is needed.

Blacks constituted 9.5 percent of the high school completions in 1975, 10.3 percent in 1980 and 10.7 percent in 1985. In 1975, 1980 and 1985, blacks constituted 8.2 percent, 9.7 percent and 10.4 percent of the enrollment in undergraduate college, respectively.

Blacks as a percent of all applicants to medical school was greater in 1985 than in 1980 and 1975. However, when compared to the total population, a higher level of parity existed in 1985 than in 1975 but was lower for 1980. The same picture was reflected when high school completions were compared. When college enrollment was considered, a lower level of parity existed for 1985 than for both 1980 and 1975. Blacks as a percent of all applicants to law school was greater in 1985 than in 1980. Higher levels of parity existed for applicants when compared to both population and high school completions during that same five years. However, the level of parity decreased for black law applicants when compared to college enrollment.

Blacks as a percent of all acceptees to medical school comprised a lower percentage in 1980 and 1975. Similarly when acceptees were compared to the standards, the level of parity in 1980 was less than in 1980 and 1975 for all three standards. Acceptance information was not available for law school.

The percent of blacks entering the first year of medical school was less in 1985 than in 1980 and 1975. Whereas the level of parity in 1985 was lower than 1980 and 1975 when comparisons were made with high school completions and undergraduate enrollment, it was higher when the population was considered.

The picture was reversed when first year entrants to law school were considered. Blacks as a percent of first year entrants comprised a larger segment in 1985 than in 1980 and 1975. However, checking the level of parity, when compared to the population, the level of parity in 1985 was lower than 1975 and equal to that of 1980. The level of parity was lower in 1985 than in 1980 and 1975 when comparisons were made with high school completions and college enrollment.

As a percent of the enrollment in medical schools, blacks comprised a greater segment in 1985 than in 1980 but a smaller segment than in 1975. Similarly, blacks enrolled in medical schools in 1985 had a lower level of parity with the population, high school completions and college enrollments in 1980 and 1975. The same picture was reflected for graduates from medical school.

As a percent of the enrollment in law schools, blacks comprised a larger segment in 1985 than in 1980 and 1975. Enrollments in law schools had a higher level of parity in 1985 than in 1980 but a lower one than 1975 when the population was compared. The same picture was revealed when high school completions were compared. Considering college enrollments, a lower level of parity existed in 1985 for enrollment in medical schools than in 1980 or 1975.

Blacks as a percentage of the graduates from professional schools comprised a smaller segment in 1985 than in 1980 and had a lower level of parity when compared to the population, high school completions and college enrollment.

Black practitioners as physicians comprised a larger segment of the practitioners in 1985 than in 1980, whereas black practitioners in law comprised a smaller segment in 1985 than in 1980 or 1975. Practitioners in medicine had a higher level of parity with the population and college enrollment in 1985 than in 1980 but a lower level when compared with high school completions. Practitioners in medicine had a lower level of parity in 1985 than in 1980 when compared with the population, high school completions and college enrollment.

In assessing the status of blacks in medicine in terms of the relative positions held related to the totals for each impacting factor between 1985 and five years earlier, black Americans in 1985 occupied an improved position on 5 of the 6 impacting factors measured. When compared to ten years earlier, black Americans in 1985 occupied an improved position on 2 of the 5 impacting factors measured (See Table 16).

In assessing the status of blacks in law in terms of the relative positions held related to the totals for each impacting factor between 1985 and five years earlier, black Americans in 1985 occupied an improved position on 4.5 of the five impacting factors measured. When compared to ten years earlier, black Americans in 1985 occupied an improved position.

When comparing the levels of parity for each impacting factor with each standard, blacks in medicine had a higher level of parity in 1985 on 2 of the 18 measures than they did five years earlier and on 2 of 15 measures than they did ten years earlier.

When comparing the levels of parity for each impacting factor with each standard, blacks in law had a higher level of parity in 1985 on 4.5 of the 15 measures than they had five years earlier and on none of the 6 measures ten years earlier.

In conclusion:

• The status of blacks in the field of medicine is more favorable than five years ago when judged on growth as a component of the totals for each status factor of the profession.

• The status of blacks in the field of medicine is less favorable today than ten years ago when judged on growth as a component of the totals for each status factor of the profession.

• The status of blacks in the field of law is more favorable today than five years ago when judged on growth as a component of the totals for each status factor of the profession.

• No status report is presented for a comparison in law for the period ten years earlier.

• The status of blacks in the field of medicine is less favorable today than it was five and ten years earlier when judged on the level of parity between factors impacting status and the standards.

• The status of blacks in the field of law is less favorable today than it was five years ago when judged on the level of parity between factors impacting status and the standards. No status report is provided for a comparison ten years earlier.

References

American Bar Association. Office of the Consultant on Legal Education, Indianapolis, Indiana, July 1986.

American Bar Association. Section of Legal Education and Admissions to the Bar, *A Review of Legal Education in the United States, Fall, 1985,* Washington, D.C.

Association of American Medical Colleges. Fall Enrollment Survey, Washington, D.C., 1986.

Association of American Medical Colleges. Office of Minority Affairs, Feb. 1986, Liaison Committee on Medical Education Questionnaire Part II, 1971–72 to 1981–82; Division of Student Services, 1982–83 to 1984–85, Washington, D.C.

Association of American Medical Colleges. Office of Minority Affairs, Washington, D.C., 1987.

Census Bureau. Current Population Reports, *Educational Attainment in the United States,* P-20, various years, and unpublished data from the March 1985 current population survey, Washington, D.C.

Census Bureau. Statistical Information Office, Population Division, Washington, D.C., 1986.

Census Bureau. *U.S. Statistical Abstract,* (1981, 1982–83, 1984, 1985, and 1986), Washington, D.C.

Law School Admissions Council (unpublished data), Washington, D.C., 1986.

Chapter IV

Geographic Mobility Status of Black Women in Higher Education Administration: Selected Parameters

Dr. Hazeltine Woods-Fouche
Title III Coordinator
Hinds Junior College District
Utica Campus, MS

Black women administrators face certain constraints and barriers to their career development. Many find the struggle to survive and advance in leadership positions a never-ending burden and challenge. Consequently, few become chief administrative officers of colleges and universities. Black women administrators employed by colleges and universities are consistently found in lower level positions with those few black women holding top-level positions concentrated at the historically black colleges and universities (HBCUs). Finlay and Crossom (1981), Tidwell (1981), Doughty (1980), Jones and Welch

(1979), among other researchers have documented the fact that although women are underrepresented in major college policy-making positions and are clustered in low-level and middle-level stereotyped administrative positions, this problem is especially severe for minority women. One possibility of improving the employment opportunity levels for black women involves their willingness to relocate to obtain an available ton-level position.

Geographic studies by Woods-Fouche (1982), Moore and Sagaria (1981), and Curby (1980) indicated that women are willing to move. Curby's study concluded that (1) women administrators demonstrated a propensity toward geographic mobility, and (2) women administrators are generally willing to make geographic changes to accept jobs for economic reasons, such as higher salary, as well as for opportunities for upward professional mobility.

Research Design

The survey sample included 326 black women administrators employed at historically black colleges and universities. Historically black colleges and universities are those institutions defined by Samuel L. Myers in his study "What is A Black College?" The black women administrators participating in the study extended over four regions: south central, middle states, north central and the Virgin Islands. Based on a directory compiled by the researcher in 1982 identifying 534 black women administrators, 550 survey questionnaires were mailed to the presidents/chancellors of the 104 historically black colleges/universities for dissemination. A total of 356 questionnaires (67 percent) was returned. Of this number, 326 (92 percent) were determined usable. Fifty-three percent of the 104 historical black colleges/universities (32 public, 23 private) participated in the study (see Appendix A). The sample questionnaire (see Appendix B) was divided into three sections: personal, educational/professional information, and factors influencing or inhibiting geographic mobility.

Results

This study of black women higher education administrators addresses issues related to their geographic mobility status for leadership advancement. The information solicited from black female higher education administrators was designed to examine the following eight research questions:

- What are the demographic and professional characteristics of black women higher education administrators on the campuses of historically black colleges/universities?
- What are the career patterns and aspirations of black women higher education administrators in top-level positions?
- If a top level position requires a change in residence, what factors related to determinants of geographic mobility motivate a person to accept the job?
- What factors related to geographic mobility do black women administrators perceive most important when a position in higher education administration is offered and a change in residence is required?
- What are the constraints to geographic mobility?
- If black women administrators would not relocate for

top-level employment, how do they rate the degree of importance of constraints related to geographic mobility and job choice for one who would consider a position requiring a change in residence?

- Are there significant differences between the mobile and immobile black women administrators in demographic characteristics, types of institutions, the rating of factors motivating as well as inhibiting a change in residence?
- If such differences do exist, what are the implications for black women aspiring for leadership positions in the profession of higher education, and how would the difference impact the recruitment of black professional women?

Although personal, educational and professional characteristics are germane to this study, the primary data included the selected factors influencing and inhibiting geographic mobility. Geographic mobility was defined as a self-reported willingness to accept another job requiring relocation of at least 150 miles one-way from one's present job site.

Of the 326 individuals participating in this study, 194 women reported themselves mobile while 132 indicated themselves immobile. The demographic characteristics solicited from participants, and analyzed by Chi-Square Test of Relationship are presented in Tables 1 through 10. The results revealed no significant difference in the groups' mobility status. The data indicated that more than 80 percent of the respondents were employed by historical black colleges and universities in the south central region. Typically, they were members of professional organizations, married, parents, and graduate degree holders. More than 60 percent of the women indicated job titles denoting middle level positions. Job

TABLE 1

Chi-Square Test of the Relationship Between Mobility Status and Age Range

Age Range	Mobile		Immobile		Age Range Totals	
	N	(%)	N	(%)	N	(%)
Under 20	5	(1.6)	1	(0.3)	6	(1.6)
20–29	12	(3.8)	1	(0.3)	13	(4.7)
30–39	77	(24.4)	35	(11.1)	112	(35.6)
40–49	62	(19.6)	35	(11.1)	97	(30.2)
50–59	25	(7.9)	44	(13.9)	69	(22.2)
60 & Over	6	(1.9)	13	(4.1)	19	(5.7)
Mobility Totals	187	(59.2)	129	(40.8)	316	(100.0)

$X^2 = 33.53483$, df $= 5$, $p < .05$ (exact probability $= .0000$)*
(No response from 10 respondents)

*significant at the given probability level

TABLE 2

Chi-Square Test of the Relationship Between Mobility Status and Marital Status

Marital Status	Mobile		Immobile		Marital Status Totals	
	N	(%)	N	(%)	N	(%)
Now Married	93	(29.2)	89	(27.9)	182	(58.4)
Never Married	40	(12.5)	17	(5.3)	57	(17.3)
Divorced	41	(12.9)	20	(6.3)	61	(18.9)
Widowed	5	(1.9)	1	(0.3)	7	(1.9)
Separated	6	(1.9)	6	(1.9)	12	(3.5)
Mobility Totals	185	(58.3)	133	(41.7)	319	(100.0)

$X^2 = 11.68650$, df $= 4$, $p < .05$ (exact probability $= .0198$)*
(No response from 7 respondents)

significant at the given probability level

TABLE 3

Chi-Square Test of the Relationship Between Mobility Status and Major Field of Study, Decade of Completion, and Highest Degree Obtained

	Mobile		Immobile		Major Field of Study Totals	
Major Field of Study	N	(%)	N	(%)	N	(%)
Education	117	(37.0)	71	(22.5)	188	(59.5)
Business	24	(7.6)	18	(5.7)	42	(13.3)
Social Sciences	17	(5.4)	12	(3.8)	29	(9.2)
Humanities/Arts	5	(1.6)	8	(2.5)	13	(4.1)
Other Sciences	17	(5.4)	19	(6.0)	36	(11.4)
Other	6	(1.9)	2	(0.6)	8	(2.5)
Mobility Totals	186	(58.9)	130	(41.1)	316	(100.0)

$X^2 = 6.04370$, df = 5, $p < .05$ (Exact probability = .3020)
(No response from 10 respondents)

Decade Of Completion	N	(%)	N	(%)	N	(%)
1950	9	(3.0)	15	(4.9)	24	(7.9)
1960	20	(6.6)	30	(9.8)	50	(16.4)
1970	88	(28.9)	58	(19.0)	146	(47.9)
1980	65	(21.3)	20	(6.6)	85	(27.9)
Mobility Totals	182	(59.7)	123	(40.3)	305	(100.0)

$X^2 = 22.93295$, df = 3, $p < .05$ (Exact probability = .0000)*
(No response from 21 respondents)

79

TABLE 3 (Continued)

Major Field of Study	Mobile		Immobile		Major Field of Study Totals	
	N	(%)	N	(%)	N	(%)
Highest Degree Obtained						
Bachelors	29	(9.0)	27	(8.4)	56	(17.3)
Masters	66	(20.4)	54	(16.7)	120	(37.2)
Specialist	10	(3.1)	2	(0.6)	12	(3.7)
Doctorate	76	(23.5)	42	(13.0)	118	(36.5)
Other	8	(2.5)	9	(2.8)	17	(5.3)
Mobility Totals	189	(58.5)	130	(41.5)	323	(100.0)

$X^2 = 17.30673$, df $= 4$, $p < .05$ (Exact probability $= .1205$)
(No response from 3 respondents)

*Significant at the given probability level

TABLE 4
Chi-Square Test of the Relationship Between Mobility Status and Type of Institution

Type of Institution	Mobile		Immobile		Type of Institution Totals	
	N	(%)	N	(%)	N	(%)
Two year Public	43	(13.7)	39	(12.5)	82	(26.0)
Four year Public	131	(41.9)	81	(25.9)	212	(67.3)
Two year Private	8	(2.6)	3	(1.0)	11	(4.1)
Four year Private	4	(1.3)	4	(1.3)	8	(2.6)
Mobility Totals	186	(59.5)	127	(40.6)	313	(100.0)

$X^2 = 3.25454$, df $= 3$, $p < .05$ (exact probability $= .3540$)
(No response from 12 respondents)

81

TABLE 5

Chi-Square Test of the Relationship Between Mobility Status and Length of Employment in Current Position

Length of Employment in Years	Mobile		Immobile		Length of Employment in Years Totals	
	N	(%)	N	(%)	N	(%)
1–5	41	(12.9)	28	(8.8)	69	(21.8)
6–10	29	(9.1)	23	(7.3)	52	(16.4)
11–15	83	(26.2)	59	(18.6)	142	(44.8)
16–20	17	(5.4)	17	(5.4)	34	(10.7)
21 and over	12	(3.8)	8	(2.5)	20	(6.3)
Mobility Totals	182	(57.4)	135	(42.6)	317	(100.0)

$X^2 = 1.05261$, df $= 4$, $p < .05$ (exact probability $= .9017$)
(No response from 9 respondents)

upward mobility within the institutions beyond middle level positions seemed to have been inevitable given that more than 80 percent indicated that they have received job promotion within their institution. Many of the administrators had been employed in these middle level positions ten years or more. Overwhelmingly, most of the women checked the item "very committed" to their current position. Data also revealed that over fifty percent of the respondents reported personal income for themselves and spouses/cohabitors not less than $30,000.

Within the sample used in this study, more than half of the women administrators indicated they had moved to accept their current position. As demonstrated in Table 6, "economic advancement," "to be near family and friends," and "professional or career advancement" were by far the predominant reasons motivating changes in geographic location to accept their current position.

TABLE 6
Factors Motivating Women
to Change Residence for
Current Position
N = 177

Motivating Factors	Frequency	Percentage*
Economic Advancement	75	23.0
Professional or Career Advancement	32	9.8
To be near Family and Friends	50	15.3
Exposure to Cultural Activities	25	7.7
Region in the United States	5	1.5
Spouse or Cohabitor's Job Opportunity	16	4.9
Other	8	2.5

*Totaled percentages exceed 100.0. Respondents could respond to any or all factors.

Demographic variables which showed significant differences were age range, marital status, decade of completion, aspiring position, and miles traveled one-way to work. These analyses revealed that women between the ages of 30 and 49 tend to be mobile. Almost all women in the immobile group were distributed in the age ranges 30–39 through 60 and over. Although the percentage variance was small (1.3%) between the married mobile and immobile women, more married women tend to be mobile. Fewer than 60 percent of the respondents received degrees in the field of education. Most of the degrees were awarded during the 1970's and 1980's. More mobile women (129) than immobile women (80) said they have changed residence for employment. While there was little difference in the distribution of women aspiring for a top level position, more mobile women than immobile women indicated aspirations for middle level positions. Most of the women (78.2%) also indicated they traveled less than 10 miles one-way to work.

The primary data for this study included seventeen selected factors identified as influencers of geographic mobility and fourteen constraints considered as inhibitors of geographic mobility. Respondents were asked to rate these factors on a seven-point scale. The data were analyzed by the t-test for independent samples to compare the mean response ratings of self-reported mobile and immobile women administrators.

Table 7 presents an analysis of seventeen factors presumably influencing geographic mobility. Of the seventeen factors rated, only three showed any significant difference. Self-reported immobile women rated "opportunities for more active social life" and "prestige, power and influence" more important than those women re-

TABLE 7

t-test for Independent Samples Comparing Mean Rating by Mobile and Immobile Women on Factors Motivating or Influencing Geographic Mobility

Factors motivating or influencing geographic mobility	Group		t	p
	Mobile Mean (N = 191)	Immobile Mean (N = 132)		
Opportunity for Advancement	1.5236	1.5758	− .41	.680
Higher Salary	1.6597	1.7348	− .61	.541
Higher Level of Administration	2.0042	2.2955	− 1.21	.227
Type of College/University	3.2094	3.0606	.58	.565
Better Schools for my Children	4.1885	3.6894	1.74	.088
Opportunities for more active Social Life	3.8691	4.6667	− 3.80	.000*
Prestige, Power and Influence	3.2356	3.8561	− 3.17	.002*
Exposure to more Cultural Opportunities	2.9476	2.8939	.28	.779
Demographic Characteristics of the Community (rural, urban, suburban, size)	2.9791	2.8788	.50	.618
Climate (weather)	2.9634	2.8636	.47	.639
Equal Job Opportunity for Spouse/Cohabitor	3.2618	2.8788	1.37	.171
Challenge of New Position	2.5812	2.4545	.63	.530
Opportunities to Conduct Research	2.9634	3.1894	− 1.17	.243
Competency and Congeniality of Colleagues	2.1623	2.3182	− .96	.337
Opportunity for Promotion	1.9319	1.9394	− .05	.961
Fringe Benefits	2.4555	2.4091	.21	.837
Region of the United States	4.0471	3.2576	2.51	.012*

*significant at the given probability level

porting themselves mobile. Mobile respondents rated "region of the United States" much higher than immobile respondents.

The rank order (based on mean ratings) of factors influencing geographic mobility by mobility status of participants is presented in Table 8. Factors were ranked from 1 (most important-highest mean score) to 17 (least important-lowest mean score). The five "most important" factors for mobile respondents were: 1) better schools for my children, 2) region of the United States, 3) opportunities for more active social life, 4) equal job opportunity for spouse/cohabitor, and 5) prestige, power and influence. The five "least important" factors were: 1) opportunity for advancement, 2) higher salary, 3) opportunity for promotion, 4) higher level of administration, and 5) competency and congeniality of colleagues. Data delineated for immobile respondents show a slight difference in rank order of the top five factors considered to be "most important." There was no difference in the rank order of constraints for those considered to be "least important" by the two groups.

A review of mobility studies revealed that age has been found to be the most firmly established determinant of geographic mobility, as age increases mobility decreases. Age was one of the fourteen selected constraints tested to determine whether there was a significant difference in the means of the two groups. As can be observed in Table 9, the mean scores for the immobile respondents were significantly higher than the mean scores of the mobile respondents on the following variables: 1) age, 2) too much pressure, 3) dependent children, 4) present tenure/job security, 5) friends, 6) spouse/cohabitor's job and 7) unwillingness of spouse/cohabitor to move.

Table 10 provides the rank order of means ratings of

86

TABLE 8

Rank Order of Motivating Factors For Mean Ratings By Mobile and Immobile Groups

Motivating Factors	Mobile	Immobile
Better Schools for My Children	1	3
Region of the United States	2	4
Opportunities for More Active Social Life	3	1
Equal Job Opportunity for Spouse/Cohabitor	4	8.5
Prestige, Power and Influence	5	2
Type of College/University	6	6
Demographic Characteristics of the Community (rural, urban, Suburban, size)	7	8.5
Opportunities to Conduct Research	8	5
Climate (weather)	8.5	10
Exposure to More Cultural Opportunities	10	7
Challenge of New Position	11	11
Fringe Benefits	12	12
Competency and Congeniality of Colleagues	13	13
Higher Level of Administration	14	14
Opportunity for Promotion	15	15
Higher Salary	16	16
Opportunity for Advancement	17	17

TABLE 9

t-test for Independent Samples Comparing Mean Ratings by Mobile and Immobile Women of Constraints to Geographic Mobility

Constraints of Geographic Mobility	Group			
	Mobile Mean (N = 191)	Immobile Mean (N = 132)	t	p
My Age	2.7696	4.0682	− 5.39	.000*
Too Much Pressure	3.2827	4.2803	− 4.31	.000*
Home Ownership/Equity	3.6230	3.8636	− .96	.336
Dependent Children	3.6230	4.2348	− 2.24	.026*
Present Tenure/Job Security	3.3979	4.1439	− 2.81	.005*
Other Dependent(s)	3.6754	4.1667	− 1.69	.091
Family Cohesiveness	3.4974	3.7576	− 1.03	.302
Friends	2.8482	3.5379	− 2.95	.003*
Lack of Encouragement from Male Peers	3.4398	3.6364	− .70	.486
Spouse/Cohabitor's Job	3.9424	4.4848	− 1.91	.058*
Expense of Moving	4.2880	4.0530	.88	.382
Unwillingness of Spouse/Cohabitor to Move	3.6283	4.3788	− 2.60	.010*
Sex Role Stereotyping	3.7382	4.2273	− 1.78	.076
Allegiance to My Current College/University	5.1570	5.8409	− 2.27	.024*

*significant at the given probability level

TABLE 10

Rank Order of Constraints for Means Ratings By Mobile and Immobile Groups

Constraints	Rank	
	Mobile	Immobile
Allegiance to my current college/university	1	1
Expense of Moving	2	10
Spouse/Cohabitor's Job	3	2
Sex role Stereotyping	4	6
Other Dependent(s)	5	7
Unwillingness of Spouse/Cohabitor to Move	6	3
Home Ownership/Equity	7.5	11
Dependent Children	7.5	5
Family Cohesiveness	9	12
Lack of Encouragement from Male Peers	10	13
Present Tenure/Job Security	11	8
Too Much Pressure	12	4
Friends	13	14
My Age	14	9

constraints to geographic mobility. Each constraint was ranked from 1 (highest mean rating) to 14 (lowest mean rating). Unlike results of factors influencing geographic mobility, ranked constraints show marked differences by mobile and immobile women. Only one constraint, "allegiance to my current college/university," received the same rank order.

Summary/Conclusions

In the aggregate, black women higher education administrators participating in this study tend to be more similar than different on variables studied. Data results show the typical respondent to reside in the south central region, to be married, to fall between the ages of thirty and forty-nine, to have at least one dependent child, to have completed her academic study in the field of education during the '70s and '80s, to be employed at a four-year public college/university in a middle level position basically acquired through promotion. Although one-hundred forty-two or more than forty percent of the administrators reported more than ten years in their current position, twenty-eight (11.2%) have a desire to move to the top of the hierarchy. Many of the respondents would relocate to reach their goal as evidenced in the number (194) reporting their mobility status to be "mobile" and the number (209) indicating that they would relocate to accept their current position. In reference to economics, approximately fifty-six percent reported salaries above $30,000.

Academically, the respondents are prepared to assume shared leadership roles in higher education administration. More than one-third (36.5%) indicated that they have been awarded the Ph.D degree, whereas, forty prcent reported having earned the masters or specialist degree. Most of the black women administrators are members or leaders of professional organizations.

A significant difference was observed on several variables. Age tended to be a deterrent to geographic mobility. As age increases, respondents' mobility status decreases. One's marital status could be a deterrent to geographic mobility, yet, almost the same number of married respondents declared themselves mobile as well as immobile. A small number of the sample is aspiring for top level positions.

The administrators are more alike than different on factors motivating or influencing geographic mobility. The self-reported immobile group rated three out of seventeen selected parameters significantly higher than the mobile group. The immobile group showed more of a need for prestige, power and influence, more active social life and to be employed in a certain region of the United States as influencers of geographic mobility. The immobile group also rated eight out of fourteen given constraints significantly higher than the mobile group. The constraint receiving the highest mean score was "allegiance to my current college/university," whereas, "my age" received the lowest mean score.

The more black women administrators become aware of and understand themselves and the higher education politics coupled with the aura of rigidity of higher education administration, the better they will be able to make career decisions which impact on their career goals. Black women have obtained academic preparedness. Now, they must be reminded that it is inside the institution itself that most administrators learn what they actually need to do on the job. Further, it is also important that black women who have leadership aspirations network with men who are still the primary decision makers.

In general, it seems apparent that a substantial proportion of black female administrators are willing to relocate in order to secure job advancement. Therefore it is imperative that black female administrators and institutions find ways to eliminate barriers or constraints to geographic mobility.

References

Aurand, C. H. and Blackburn, R. T. Career patterns and job mobility of college and university music faculty *Journal of Research in Music Education,* 1973, 21, 162–168.

Benton, Sandra Kay York. Reported factors influencing the selection of women to top-level administrative positions in public.

Community Colleges. Unpublished doctoral dissertation, The University of Tennessee, 1979.

Bogue, D. J. A methodological study of migration and labor mobility in Michigan and Ohio in 1947. Oxford, Ohio: Scripps, 1949.

Brown, Andolyn Virginia. Black female administrators in higher education. A survey of demographic data, previous work experience, characteristics of employing institutions. An Unpublished doctoral dissertation, Bowling Green State University, 1980.

Curby, Vicki Morgan. *Woman administrators in higher education: their geographic mobility.* Ruth Strong Research Award Monograph Series: No. 4. National Association of Women Deans, Administrators and Counselors, 1980.

Dejoie, Carolyn M. The black woman in alienation in white academia. *Negro Educational Review,* XXVII, No. 1 (January, 1977), 4–13.

Despite gains, women, minority—group members lag in college jobs. *Chronicle of Higher Education,* (February 3, 1982), 4.

Doughty, Rosie. The black female administrator: Woman in a double bind. in *Leadership.* Lexington Books, 1980.

Finlay, Charyl Schratz, Crosson, Patricia H. Woman in higher education administration: Status and strategies. *Administrative Update*. Volume 2, No. 3, 1981.

Galloway, L. E. Geographic mobility in the United States 1957 to 1960. Washington, D.C.: United States Department of Health Education and Welfare, 1969.

Ladkinsky, J. The geographic mobility of professional and technical manpower. *The Journal of Human Resources*, 1967, 2. 475–494.

Lansing, John B. and Morgan, James N. The effect of geographic mobility on income. *The Journal of Human Resources*, Volume 2, No. 4, Fall 1967, 449–460.

Turner, William H. and Michael, John A. *Traditionally black institutions of higher education: Their identification and selected characteristics*. National Center for Education Statistics, U.S. Governmental Printing Office, Washington, D.C.: 1978.

Watson, Bernard C. The black administrator in higher education: Current dilemmas, problems and opportunities. (Philadelphia: Temple University Press), April, 1972.

Weber, Margaret B. and others. Why women are underrepresented in educational administration. *Educational Leadership*, Volume 38, No. 4, January, 1981.

Woods-Fouche, Hazeltine. Selected parameters of potential geographic mobility of black women in higher education administration at traditionally black public colleges and universities. An Unpublished Ph.D. Dissertation, Kansas State University, 1982.

Appendix A
Participating Historical Black Colleges and Universities

Alabama State University
Albany State College
Allen University
Atlanta University
Benedict College
Bethune Cookman College
Bishop College
Bowie State College
Central State University
Cheyney University
Clark College
Coahoma Junior College
College of the Virgin Islands
Delaware State College
Elizabeth City State
 University
Fayetteville State University

Florida A&M University
Fort Valley State College
Grambling State University
Howard University
Jackson State University
Jarvis Christian College
Johnson C. Smith University
Kentucky State University
Lane College
Lawson State Community
 College
LeMoyne-Owen College
Lincoln University, MO
Lincoln University-PA
Meharry Medical College
Miles College
Morris Brown College

Morris College
Morristown College
North Carolina A&T State
North Carolina Central
  University
Oakwood College
Paine College
Paul Quinn College
Prairie View A&M College
Shaw University
South Carolina State College
Southern University System-
  Baton Rouge
Southwestern Christian
  College

St. Augustine's College
Stillman College
S.D. Bishop State Junior
  College
Texas Southern University
Tuskegee Institute
University of Arkansas at
  Pine Bluff
University of the District of
  Columbia
Voorhees College
Wilberforce University
Winston-Salem State College

Appendix B

Administrative Perception Scale (on Black Women in Higher Education Administration)

PART 1. PERSONAL, EDUCATION AND PROFES-
SIONAL INFORMATION (To be completed by
all respondents)

Please check the item most applicable to you for each of
the following:

(1) AGE

___ under 20
___ 20–29
___ 30–39
___ 40–49
___ 50–59
___ 60–

(2) Marital Status

___ Now married
___ Never married
___ Divorced
___ Widowed
___ Separated
___ Other (please specify)

___ _____

(3) Children Under 6 Years of Age

   __ None
   __ One
   __ Two or more

(4) Children 6–11 of Age

   __ None
   __ One
   __ Two
   __ Three
   __ Four or more

(5) OTHER DEPENDENT(S)

   __ Yes
   __ No

(6) Please indicate the degree(s) you have earned by checking the space provided and by specifying the major field of study. Also, indicate year of each degree completion and the degree awarding institution.

Degrees	Major Field of Study	Year Completed	College or University
__ BA/BS	_____	_____	_____
__ MA/MS	_____	_____	_____
__ Ed.S	_____	_____	_____
__ Ph.D	_____	_____	_____
__ Other	_____	_____	_____

(7) Please check the type of institution of which you are currently employed.

   __ Two-year public   __ Four-year public
   __ Two year private   __ Four year private

(8) What is your current job title? _____

(9) How did you obtain this position? Check applicable response(s).

   __ Recruited __ Referred __ Promoted __ Transferred
   __ Other (specify) _____

(10) How long have you been employed in your current position?

   __ 1–5 years __ 6–10 years __ 11–15 years __ over 20 years

(11) Did your current position require you to change residence?
___ Yes ___ No. If yes, please rank any or all of the applicable factors listed below which motivated you to move:

___ economic advancement
___ professional or career advancement
___ to be near family and friends
___ exposure to cultural activities
___ region of the United States
___ spouse or cohabitor's job opportunity
___ other (please specify) _____

(12) What was your most recent previous employment position (job title)? _____

(13) Please indicate the position (job title) you would see yourself being most likely to seek for your next promotion: _____

(14) To what degree are you committed to your current position?
___ very committed   ___ somewhat committed
___ somewhat uncommitted

(15) What is your salary range: Check the one most applicable.
___ Less than $10,000   ___ $25,000–29,999
___ $15,000–19,999   ___ $30,000–34,999
___ $20,000–24,999   ___ $35,000–and over

(16) If applicable, what is your spouse or cohabitor's salary range? Check the one most applicable.
___ Less than $10,000   ___ $25,000–29,999
___ $15,000–19,999   ___ $30,000–34,999
___ $20,000–24,999   ___ $35,000–and over
                          ___ Net applicable

(17) Do you or own or have equity in your home? ___ Yes ___ No

(18) What is the approximate distance (miles) you travel to work one-way? _____

(19) Please list the professional organizations of which you are a member. Please write out the identifying word. in full.

_____

_____

_____

_____

_____

PART II. DIRECTIONS: If you would consider moving to accept a top level position in higher education administration, please complete this section. If you would not relocate, GO TO PART III.

(20) If you had an opportunity to become employed in a top level position such as president, vice president, dean, at cetera in higher education administration and the job change required you to move at least a distance of 150 miles one-way, on a 1 to 7 scale rate by circling the number corresponding to the factors listed below which best describe the degree of importance you feel necessary to consider when a job change requires you to move.

	Extremely Important			Neutral			Not Important At All
Opportunity for advancement	1	2	3	4	5	6	7
Higher salary	1	2	3	4	5	6	7
Higher level of administration	1	2	3	4	5	6	7
Type of college or university	1	2	3	4	5	6	7
Better schools for my children	1	2	3	4	5	6	7
Opportunities for more active social life	1	2	3	4	5	6	7
Prestige, power and influence	1	2	3	4	5	6	7

	Extremely Important		Neutral			Not Important At All
Exposure to more cultural opportunities	1	2	3	4	5	6	7
Demographic characteristics of the community (rural, urban, suburban, size)	1	2	3	4	5	6	7
Climate (weather)	1	2	3	4	5	6	7
Equal job opportunity for spouse or cohabitor	1	2	3	4	5	6	7
Challenge of new position	1	2	3	4	5	6	7
Opportunities to conduct research	1	2	3	4	5	6	7
Competency and congeniality of colleagues	1	2	3	4	5	6	7
Opportunity for promotion	1	2	3	4	5	6	7
Fringe benefits	1	2	3	4	5	6	7
Region of the United States	1	2	3	4	5	6	7
Other (please specify and rate) ___	1	2	3	4	5	6	7

(21) Given the constraints below, rate the factors on a 1 to 7 scale you consider most inhibiting to a job change requiring relocation. (A rating of 1—least inhibiting and a rating of 7—most inhibiting.) Circle the appropriate number for each factor.

	Least Inhibiting						Most Inhibiting
My age	1	2	3	4	5	6	7
Too much pressure	1	2	3	4	5	6	7
Home ownership or equity	1	2	3	4	5	6	7

	Least Inhibiting					Most Inhibiting
Dependent children						
1	2	3	4	5	6	7
Present tenure or job security						
1	2	3	4	5	6	7
Other dependant(s)						
1	2	3	4	5	6	7
Family cohesiveness						
1	2	3	4	5	6	7
Friends						
1	2	3	4	5	6	7
Lack of encouragement from male peers						
1	2	3	4	5	6	7
Spouse or cohabitor's job						
1	2	3	4	5	6	7
Expense of moving						
1	2	3	4	5	6	7
Unwillingness of spouse or cohabitor to move						
1	2	3	4	5	6	7
Sex role sterotyping						
1	2	3	4	5	6	7
Allegiance to my current college or university						
1	2	3	4	5	6	7
Other (please specify and rate)						
1	2	3	4	5	6	7
_____						
1	2	3	4	5	6	7

PART III. DIRECTIONS: If you would not relocate to accept a top level position in higher education administration, please complete this section.

(22) Listed below are several conditions often considered in the change of job requiring relocation. Please indicate the degree of importance you deem necessary for one who is anticipating moving to acquire a top level position in higher education admin-istration. Please rate each condition by circling the appropriate number.

	Extremely Important		Neutral			Not Important At All	
Opportunity for advancement	1	2	3	4	5	6	7
Higher salary	1	2	3	4	5	6	7
Higher level of administration	1	2	3	4	5	6	7
Type of college or university	1	2	3	4	5	6	7
Better schools for my children	1	2	3	4	5	6	7
Opportunities for more active social life	1	2	3	4	5	6	7
Prestige, power and influence	1	2	3	4	5	6	7
Exposure to more cultural opportunities	1	2	3	4	5	6	7
Demographic characteristics of the community (rural, urban, suburban, size)	1	2	3	4	5	6	7
Climate (weather)	1	2	3	4	5	6	7
Equal job opportunity for spouse or cohabitor	1	2	3	4	5	6	7
Challenge of new position	1	2	3	4	5	6	7
Opportunities to conduct research	1	2	3	4	5	6	7
Competency and congeniality of colleagues	1	2	3	4	5	6	7
Opportunity for promotion	1	2	3	4	5	6	7
Fringe benefits	1	2	3	4	5	6	7
Region of the United States	1	2	3	4	5	6	7
Other (please specify and rate) ____	1	2	3	4	5	6	7

(23) One may consider the factors listed below as consstraints to moving to accept a top level position in higher education admin-

istration. On a scale of 1 to 7 to what degree do you feel the constraints inhibit one to move to accept the job.

	Least inhibiting					Most Inhibiting	

Age

1	2	3	4	5	6	7

Too much pressure

1	2	3	4	5	6	7

Home ownership or equity

1	2	3	4	5	6	7

Dependent children

1	2	3	4	5	6	7

Present tenure or job security

1	2	3	4	5	6	7

Other dependant(s)

1	2	3	4	5	6	7

Family cohesiveness

1	2	3	4	5	6	7

Friends

1	2	3	4	5	6	7

Lack of encouragement from male peers
Spouse or cohabitor's job

1	2	3	4	5	6	7

Expense of moving

1	2	3	4	5	6	7

Unwillingness of spouse or cohabitor to move
Sex role stereotyping

1	2	3	4	5	6	7

Allegiance to my current college or university
Other (please specify and rate)

1	2	3	4	5	6	7

_____

1	2	3	4	5	6	7

THANK YOU FOR YOUR HELP. PLEASE FEEL
FREE TO MAKE COMMENTS CONCERNING THIS
STUDY.

Return completed questionnaire in the self-addressed,
stamped envelope to:

Dr. Hazeltine
Woods-Fouché
Utica Junior
College
Utica, MS 39175

NAFEO

The National Association for Equal Opportunity in Higher Education, (NAFEO), founded in October, 1969, was formed as a voluntary, independent association by historically and predominantly black colleges and universities. It is organized to articulate the need for a higher education system where race, income, and previous education are not determinants of either the quantity or quality of higher education. This is an association of those colleges and universities which are not only committed to this ultimate goal, but are now fully committed in terms of their resources, human and financial, to achieving that goal.

The Association proposes, through collective efforts of its membership, to promote the widest possible sensitivity to the complex factors involved in and the institutional commitment required for creating successful higher education programs for students from groups buffeted by racism and neglected by economic, educational and social institutions of America.

To achieve this goal, NAFEO has determined the following priorities:

1. To provide a unified framework representing historically black colleges and similarly situated institutions in their attempt to continue as viable forces in American society;

2. To build the case for securing increased support from federal agencies, philanthropic foundations and other sources;

3. To increase the active participation of Black in the leadership of educational organizations together with memberships on Federal boards and commissions relating to education; and

4. To provide detailed, continuing yearly analyses of constructive information about these colleges and to use that information to help the public develop and maintain a sensitivity to the overall needs of these institutions of higher education.

NAFEO's aim is to increase the flow of students from minority and economically deprived families, mostly Black, into the mainstream of our society.

In carrying out its four major specific objectives, NAFEO serves as a—

1. Voice for Historically Black Colleges

2. Clearinghouse of Information on Black Colleges

3. Coordinator in Black Higher Education

4. Presidential Resource.

The National Association for Equal Opportunity in Higher Education represents the historically and predominantly black colleges and universities of this nation.

There are some 117 NAFEO institutions, consisting of private 2-year and 4-year institutions, public 2-year and 4-year institutions, as well as graduate and professional schools located in fourteen southern states, six northern states, four mid-west and western states, the Virgin Islands and the District of Columbia. These institutions enroll upwards of 250,000 students and graduate more than 40,000 students annually with undergraduate, graduate and professional degrees. Since 1966, these institutions have awarded a half million undergraduate, graduate and professional degrees. They are the providers of equal educational opportunity with attainment and productivity for thousands of students.

NAFEO'S RESEARCH ADVISORY COMMITTEE

Dr. Gregory R. Anrig
President
Educational Testing Service (ETS)
Princeton, NJ 08541

Dr. Alexander W. Astin
Professor and Director
Higher Education Research Institute
Graduate School of Education
University of California
Los Angeles, CA 90024

Dr. Elias Blake, Jr.
Former President
Clark College
240 Chestnut Street, S.W.
Atlanta, GA 30314

Dr. Ernest L. Boyer
President
The Carnegie Foundation for the
Advancement of Teaching
5 Ivy Lane
Princeton, NJ 08540

Dr. Richard L. Ferguson
Executive Vice President
American College Testing (ACT)
2201 N. Dodge Street
P.O. Box 168
Iowa City, IA 52243

Dr. Alan H. Kirschner
Director
Department of Research & Government
Affairs
United Negro College Fund, Inc.
500 East 62nd Street
New York, NY 10021

Dr. Charles "A" Lyons, Jr.
Former Chancellor
Fayetteville State University
Fayetteville, NC 28301-4298

Mrs. Carol Hobson Smith
Former Staff Director, National Advisory
Committee on Blacks in HI ED and Black
Colleges and Universities
4801 Queens Chapel Terrace, N.E.
Washington, DC 20017

Dr. Joffre T. Whisenton
President
Southern University System
Baton Rouge, LA 70813

Dr. Mary Carter-Williams
Coordinator, Continuing Education and
Community Service Programs
School of Communications
Howard University
Washington, DC 20059

Dr. Reginald Wilson
Director
Office of Minority Concerns
American Council on Education
One Dupont Circle
Washington, DC 20036-1193

110